From Horses to Chieftains
WITH THE 8TH HUSSARS

SECOND EDITION
published in 2002
by
WOODFIELD PUBLISHING
Woodfield House, Babsham Lane, Bognor Regis
West Sussex PO21 5EL, England.

ISBN 1-873203-17-9

From Horses to Chieftains

WITH THE 8TH HUSSARS
1934-1959

RICHARD NAPIER

Woodfield

THE BAND OF THE 15/19TH HUSSARS. SHORNCLIFF CHURCH PARADE, 1934

This story dedicated to the servicemen who fought in World War II; they came from all walks of life, yet in a short space of time became sailors, soldiers, or airmen. God bless them all.

L/CPL MOUNT ON THE DRUMHORSE – 1936.

Contents

REGIMENTAL GUARD OF HONOUR AT THE WEDDING OF 8TH HUSSARS STALWART, MAJOR 'JUMBO' PHILLIPS, IN 1950.

Foreword

by General Sir John W. Hackett
GCB, KCB, CB, CBE, MBE, DSO*, MC

IT IS SOMETIMES SAID, PERHAPS A LITTLE PERVERSELY, that the
British Army does not really exist, that it is in fact no more
than a collection of individual corps and regiments loosely
gathered together into one somewhat incoherent whole. If
this is said to emphasise the rugged individuality of the
separate regimental components there is much truth in it. An
officer, for example, is not normally commissioned into 'The
Army', although a so-called 'general list' has been useful in
furnishing a convenient category for certain rather special
cases. An officer is usually commissioned into a particular
regiment or corps and a man joined up in the ranks is asked
to specify what regiment he would like to join. Considerable
care is then taken, if he has a preference, to see that he goes
where he wants to. The individual component units of the
Service, of course, are integrated into one immense whole,
whose management, support, supply, training and command
are laid down by its constitutional masters. The regimental
parts, however, preserve a high degree of independence and
make a considerable point of demonstrating their separate-

ness from the others. The Royal Navy and the Royal Air Force have, and deserve, appellations which imply a completeness within an integrated whole, whose members expect to be moved as occasion demands from one part of it to another, from a ship or a squadron to some other ship or squadron. The corporate loyalty developed within these units can be very high but does not dominate the outlook of the individual member to the degree to which membership of a regiment does in the Army. The case for re-designating the British Army the Royal British Army would find only limited support.

As a result of this tendency, not uniquely displayed in the Army of Great Britain but more highly developed there, probably, than in the army of any other major power, the regiment develops a strong likeness to a family. Nowhere has this been more so than in the cavalry regiments and never was it more powerfully evident than before the cavalry lost its horses and was mechanised. The fact that the life of a cavalry regiment was arranged, as it were, around the horse gave it a unity, an almost inward-turning tendency, more marked in cavalry regiments than in units of other arms. The horse was a living creature requiring constant and careful attention, and its interests were in horsed units of paramount importance. This meant, for one example, that in one of these you could never put up the shutters and have a complete holiday. It used to be a matter of a sometimes slightly sour jest among cavalry soldiers that, whereas in the infantry battalion next door the celebration of some event of historic importance could be marked by a complete holiday this, for us, was never possible. The troop stables had to be mucked out early in the morning and the overnight bedding piled to one side. The troop horses, whatever the season or weather, had every day to be got out on exercise, one ridden and the rider leading one or two others, and then brought in again. They had to be groomed and their minor ailments attended to. They had to be fed and watered several times during the day, until their bedding was restored to the stable floors in the evening and they were given their ration of hay and bedded down for the night. The night guards would then take over the supervision of the stables, from the stable guards who were on duty during the day, and the orderly officer would be doing the rounds of the stables towards midnight. During the day the saddlery and other equipment required in the use and management of the horse had to be maintained and kept clean and in working order. There might be no parade in the normal use of that term upon a day which was designated as a holiday, but the appearance in orders of the phrase 'the rest of the day will be observed as a holiday' was greeted, if it aroused any comment at all, with cynical and probably impolite comment.

This book, written by someone who is far from being a professional writer, opens a window on this family world and conveys a lively and truthful impression of what it was like to be a member of such a family, on service at home or abroad, in peace and in war. It covers the transition from the world of the horse to the wholly different and at first completely bewildering world of armed service without it. I knew the author pretty well, from the time our paths first crossed at the beginning of the thirties. He was a trim, smart, nice looking and lively lad whose boy's service led on into a good many years of membership of this particular family. He was a band boy to begin with and continued on in men's service as a member of the band. The mere existence of regimental bands, by the way, is as significant as is variety in dress and behaviour (the term 'uniform' means in some respects quite the reverse of what would appear to be its normal meaning: the uniform of one regiment would be in some details unacceptable in another) of the fiercely protected individuality of the regiments themselves. The band, in peace, was an indispensable part of the regiment's separate existence. It played on all appropriate occasions the regimental march, along with all its other music, and in the case of this particular regiment the playing of the regimental march was always followed, for example when the band played in the officer's mess at the close of dinner, by a rendering of the hymn 'Abide With Me'. This was said to have originated in an act of punishment upon the regiment for improper behaviour somewhere, at some time (very few people could tell you when or where, except that it was in the distant past on service somewhere abroad) in a convent. The regiment, when anyone thought about it, was pleased with its band and proud of it but took largely for granted the high standard of performance which was expected of it. In some ways it could almost be regarded as the core and kernel of the regiment, an outstanding demonstration of its individuality and distinction from others.

In wartime the band puts its instruments down and acts as part of the casualty-handling arrangements, furnishing stretcher bearers and the like.

This book looks at the regiment through the eyes of a member of the band, occupying over the years a unique position to live the regiment's own separate life and observe its idiosyncrasies. It makes a good story, simply told. It also throws a light of some penetration upon an unusual and now only dimly remembered institution, a horsed cavalry regiment in the British Army.

CAVALRY HORSES AND STAFF CAR – EGYPT 1935.

THE AUTHOR – SHORNCLIFF, 1934

CHAPTER 1

Boy Soldier

I WAS BORN ON A COLD, DISMAL DAY in November in the year 1919, without pomp or ceremony. I had been conceived out of wedlock and my arrival had been most embarrassing to my mother. There were no State benefits for unmarried mothers in those days so my mother, having been deserted by her Australian boyfriend, had to seek means of supporting me somehow. In sheer desperation she contacted The Foundling Hospital School – an Institution existing solely for the benefit of 'waifs and strays', founded by Thomas Coram and supported purely on the benevolence of voluntary contributions.

When only just a few months old I was handed over into their care and placed with a wonderful foster family, who brought me up as their own until I reached the age of five. Not only did they receive me but they had, over a period of ten years, five other boys and girls fostered out to them from the Foundling Hospital. They remained my father and mother until their deaths and their own children, Don and Louise, remain my brother and sister to this day. In later life, I naturally wondered about my humble origins and sought to find the facts of my real father and mother. I learned that my mother was a nursemaid in London at the end of the 1914–18 War and my Father was an Australian soldier stationed in the UK on his last fling before being posted back to his homeland. Mother never heard from him again. He just disappeared into oblivion.

At the age of five, in 1924, I was reluctantly returned to the Foundling Hospital School in Bloomsbury Square in London. It was a sad day for us all, especially once dressed in the school uniform and giving my clothes back to my parents. Amid lots of tears we said our goodbyes and they were gone. I had arrived at the Big School! For a long time they had talked of nothing else and now it had come. I didn't quite know whether I liked it or not!

Here, I was to get a good grounding in military discipline along with 200 other boys and 150 girls. After living in a tiny cottage, the sheer size of the school was overwhelming at first sight. It had it's own chapel, hospital, gymnasium and sports-ground; a huge dining-hall plus the classrooms and dormitories which, for a while, was very bewildering to a five-year-old, but I soon settled down and enjoyed my schooldays to the full. Once a month was 'Visiting Day' when our parents came to see us. For the first few months I wept bitterly when they left but soon got used to the routine. The educational standards were very good and any exceptional children would be sent for higher education once the necessary examinations were passed. The curriculum included music and carpentry for the boys and cooking and music for the girls, with a strong emphasis on all sorts of sports.

I was to experience a further upheaval two years later when in 1926 the whole school moved en-bloc to new premises and took over the St Anne's School in Redhill, Surrey. This had many advantages in that we had large playing fields adjacent to the London-to-Brighton railway lines, which opened up the hobby of train spotting of the famous steam engines for us boys. The new school was also situated in a beautiful rural area where we were able to go on nature study walks.

In preparation for the changeover the older children had been rehearsing for weeks ready for the march through London to Waterloo Station, preceded by the school band. We, Infants, followed behind in coaches and the event created much interest from the Londoners. I was to stay here for the rest of my schooling. I tried my hand at everything but succeeded best with music, so at the age of ten I joined the school band as a Band Cadet. Needless to say, it was a military band and as school bands go it was of a very high standard. The Bandmaster was a Captain Owen, ex-Metropolitan Police Director of Music. Several of our boys went on to the Royal Military Academy, Kneller Hall, later to become Bandmaster in their own right, whilst a few attained the distinction of becoming Directorates of Music, with a Rank of Major. Yes, music was taken very seriously indeed at our school and after a year, at the age of eleven years, I was in the band proper and at thirteen I was on the Solo Clarinet Stand. I thoroughly enjoyed my music, so much so that on a Wednesday afternoon when nearly all the other boys were out in the playing fields, I would volunteer to go to music practice. So keen was I that the Bandmaster gave me a second instrument - the E flat Saxophone. This was a rare occurrence.

Every summer, special trains were booked to take the entire school, lock, stock and barrel, for a camping holiday at Folkestone, Kent. The only members of staff not to be included were the caterers; these would be hired from a nearby Army camp – professional Army chefs. The senior boys were responsible for erecting the tents and the senior girls for the filling and stitching of the mattresses and pillows. The annual camp was on farmlands very near the Shorncliffe Military Barracks from where the Army chefs came to cook our meals on the outside traditional ranges.

Although on holiday, our religious education continued and every Sunday we would either have a 'Drum-head' service in the camp or else we would march with the band to the parish church in the town some three miles away. This created great interest with the local population who enjoyed our visits to their church. In either case, the band played a vital part.

We would often get visits from 'Old Boys' who would be stationed at Shorncliffe. On one occasion we had a mounted display come to our camp to entertain us. The Regiment was the 4th/7th Dragoon Guards and in their programme was a 'tent-pegging' display. This would entail riders on horseback at full gallop lifting tent pegs from the ground with their lances, whilst a man with a protective shield on his back bent over the peg, which was placed between his legs, who was dressed up as a clown, which went down well with us children. We watched the riders perform and were thrilled with their exploits when, suddenly, something went desperately wrong. The clown on this time round failed to get up on his feet after supposedly being knocked down by the rider. A silent hush descended; we stood and waited but still he remained on the ground,. At last, realising something was wrong, our Chaplain went over to him. He had been accidentally stabbed in the spine. An ambulance was brought and he was removed to hospital and the show discontinued. We were all very upset. We were to learn later that the man had remained paralysed and was discharged from the Service.

The musicians turned out from our school were of a very high calibre. Any Regiment in the British Army in need of boy musicians would apply to our school and their requirements were usually met. That is how I joined the 8th Kings' Royal Irish Hussars and became a boy soldier.

School days passed all too quickly and when I became 14 years old I was informed by the Headmaster that I would be joining the Army in the 8th Hussars, if I passed my medical, of course. I was to report to the Recruiting Centre at Whitehall to be medically examined by their MO. His first reaction on seeing me was to break out in fits of laughter; I wondered what the hell was wrong. Eventually he said

'How old are you?'

'Fourteen' I replied.

'How tall are you?'

'Four foot, four and a half inches, Sir.'

'How much do you weigh?'

'Five and a half stone, Sir.'

'Well,' says he, 'you'd better go back where you came from and literally grow up.' And, as if in after thought, he continued 'And put on some more weight.'

My mate, who passed his medical and I, along with the master who accompanied us, returned to school with the

Medical Officer's report and things carried on much as usual except my food, which I noticed had increased twofold; also the Bandmaster gave me extra tuition on the Clarinet because, he said, I should concentrate on that and have the Saxophone as a secondary instrument. I preferred the Sax, but I took his advice.

This continued for six months when I once again went off to Whitehall for another attempt to join His Majesty's Army. This time the MO, who recalled my previous visit, carried out the medical with a smirk on his face. I guessed he had been asked to pass me if my general health was satisfactory. He had almost finished when he looked at my teeth. Now one of my upper front teeth was broken and had grown across the other, leaving the corner of the break uppermost against my top lip. This meant that any pressure applied to my lip would result in my lip being cut. 'What instrument do you play?' he asked. 'The clarinet, Sir' I replied. There was a moment's pause then he remarked 'Providing you don't play a brass instrument, I can let you in.' then he signed my certificate.

I returned to school rather excited. I had made it! I was also apprehensive, for although I was looking forward to the challenge of a new life, I began now to wonder just what it would entail. After all, my life hitherto had been very sheltered and secluded; ahead now lay change and challenge. It was on 10th October 1934 (this date I was to repeat thousands of times during the next thirty years) I finally left school and joined the 8th KRI Hussars, Cavalry of the Line.

My first destination was the Recruiting Centre at Whitehall, where my mate and I were accommodated overnight before entraining for Shorncliffe, Kent, the following morning. Well, here we were out on our own for the first time ever with the Recruiting Centre all hustle and bustle and populated by giants (or so it appeared to us). The Grenadier Guardsmen on sentry duties were so tall and when they sprang from their sentry boxes to start on their beats I just ran for my life, which caused much amusement amongst the older soldiers. Imagine! I was only four feet, five inches high and the sentries in their bearskins with fixed bayonets were to me an awesome sight; they appeared miles high!

My mate, Spike, (so to be nicknamed soon) and I were told to report to the office at 8 a.m. In the meantime, we were free to do as we pleased. Never having been on our own before, we were somewhat scared to go anywhere, so we found a canteen in the building, had a cup of tea and I bought my first packet of cigarettes. These were to get me into trouble in the very near future. I hadn't realised that, being a Boy Soldier, I was governed by very strict rules and regulations until the age of eighteen when I would graduate on the Man's Service. We decided to go for a walk so we tidied up our school uniforms, which was a strange sight to any who had not seen it before. It consisted of chocolate brown jacket and trousers, scarlet waistcoat with brass buttons, and a large starched collar outside the jacket with a big ribbon bow. The cap was a brown and scarlet side-hat. So dressed, we stepped out into the world and on to the streets of London.

We didn't go far for fear of getting lost in the dark, so we decided to just go round the block. After two or three times on this circuit and two cigarettes, we agreed to call it a day and so we returned to the land of the giants!

We had supper and went to bed but sleep didn't come easy mainly because of the noise from the big hall downstairs. All too soon, morning came and the excitement of a train journey to Shorncliffe, Kent. We had travelled this route often on our way to our summer holiday camp at Folkestone. We chatted excitedly about our new found freedom and of the exciting future that lay ahead. The 8th Hussars were stationed at present in Egypt so we were to be temporarily attached to the 15th/19th Hussars in Shorncliffe, until such times as we could sail for Egypt.

CHAPTER 2

Shorncliffe

The train journey to Shorncliffe was most enjoyable in that we were free of supervision for the first time in our lives. Admittedly, we raised quite a few eyebrows as we mingled with other passengers, being so conspicuously dressed, but we managed to take this in our stride and made the most of the occasion.

We were met at the station and taken on to Lawrence Barracks and directly to the Bandroom. There we met the NCO in charge of Boys and we were introduced to about ten other Boys. We were allotted a bed and then taken to the Cookhouse for a lunch. Again, our school uniforms very soon became the talking point and of course my height. I was immediately nicknamed 'Titch' and this name was to stick to me throughout my entire Army career.

We eagerly devoured our lunch, which consisted of some huge thick slices of bread, a pat of butter and a massive chunk of cheese. After being given a knife, we were told to 'get stuck in'; this was followed by a mug of tea, which I could hardly lift and a dish of prunes and custard to round off. After we had satisfied our hunger and thirst we had instructions to return to the Bandroom where I got into my first spot of bother over those cigarettes I had bought in London.

On entering the Bandroom the NCO in charge of Boys called me over and for his records asked my name and number followed by

'Do you smoke?'

I was about to answer 'Yes' when my eye caught sight of a Boy vigorously shaking his head indicating me to say no. Almost before I got it out a hand flashed out and struck me a fourpenny one on the face.

'That's for lying,' he said.

I cried. I hadn't realised that he had gone through my suitcase whilst I was in the cookhouse and found my packet of 'fags'. Apparently, smoking was strictly forbidden for Boys and I was to learn many other rules before very long. For instance, it didn't take me long to learn that a Boy's life in the Army was a dog's life – almost Dickensian. The rules had to be strictly adhered to. They were:

No Smoking! No Swearing! No Drinking!
No going to the NAAFI except for one hour only in the evening!
No going out of Barracks without permission!
No communicating verbally with any of the men in the regiment except the Bandsmen!
No wearing of Civilian Clothes!

Also, all Boys were to be in bed by 9.30pm every night, with their boots cleaned, buttons polished and all their kit for the morning laid out for inspection by the NCO, who would appear precisely at 9.30pm and make his rounds. Should anything not come up to his standards, the offending Boy would be kicked out of bed and made to clean his kit again. He would also be put on 'Report' and that would invariably mean extra fatigue duties and in a Cavalry Regiment that would entail some very hard chores indeed. If I had any romantic ideas of a soldier's life, they were soon dashed after I had completed my first day. This is the programme that had so effectively brought me down to earth:

05.30 hours	REVEILLE
05.45 hours	Physical Training (after having washed and shaved in cold water) (I was excused this first Parade because I had no P.T. kit)
06.00 hours	Stables : watering and mucking out
08.00 hours	Breakfast
09.00 hours	First Band Parade; Room inspection and kit inspection, then for Band Personnel band practice for the rest of the day.

My day, however, was somewhat different. Spike and I were first paraded before the Bandmaster for an introduction, then on to the Squadron Leader and at twelve noon an introduction to the Commanding Officer via the RSM (Regimental Sergeant Major). All this time I was in a cold sweat not knowing whether I was coming or going, still in my school uniform and not realising just how peculiar I looked, standing just four feet five inches tall. These cavalry men must have thought I had stepped out of a Dickens' novel!

The afternoon was another experience. After lunch we were sent to the Quartermaster to be kitted out. At last, I thought, I'd be able to get out of school uniform. I was becoming increasingly aware just how odd I looked and I did so want to be in my soldier's uniform. When I entered the QM Store, the Storeman couldn't see me because his counter was five feet high – but we got round that. Having ascertained my name, rank and number he began to issue the kit. First, the kit-bag, which stood taller than me, then came all the kit and equipment normally issued to a cavalry man, which included a cut-throat razor; of course, I didn't shave yet but it was presumed that one day I would!

During the morning I had been issued with a list of instructions and told many things, one of them being my pay. I learned that all the time I was on Boys' Service I would be paid one shilling (5p) per day. At the time I thought I was in heaven having all that money, with full board into the bargain, including my clothes to come at the end of the week, but I soon found it to be otherwise.

Back to the QM, when it came to fitting me out with uniform it was no surprise that there was nothing to fit me, except the cap. Now this cap was the regular army issue, but being a cavalry regiment they had their own type. I was instructed to throw my issued one in the bin outside and to go to the tailors and purchase a regimental one at the cost of 7/6d. I was already in debt, but at least there was no interest charge for credit! Because there was no uniform to fit me, I was sent to the tailor who was to make me a complete outfit of two jackets, two pairs of slacks, and two pairs of riding breeches – the cost was £15, of which I would only be charged £5. My debt was growing. With these charges already levied against me, plus a monthly charge for barrack damages, a charge for The Regimental Association and a Charge for Widows and Orphans, I was dead up against it before I had even started! Then I realised that to pay back what I owed, plus other expenses that I might incur, I might as well sign on for twenty-one years for I felt certain, right now, that it would take all that time and more possibly before I even became solvent. However, I had only signed on for a period of nine years with the Colours plus three years on the Reserve, to become effective only when I graduated on to Man's Service at the age of 18. Financially I was feeling 'up against it'.

I came out of the QM Store with two sets of two-piece overalls, which were commonly called 'Canvas', and these with a fair bit of doctoring by the tailor and shrinking were to be my dress until the time khaki uniforms were ready. At last! I got out of my school uniform and was now a fully fledged Boy Soldier.

My first task was to clean up my kit and here I received help and advice, from the older Boys who all seemed keen to help me settle in. The boots, for instance, the famous, traditional Army boots, when new arrived covered in a protective grease. This had to be removed and the boots polished in the shortest possible time. This was done by a 'burning method', with a lighted candle, care being taken not to burn the chrome leather, which had a mottled surface. This was smoothed out by a 'boning process' using a toothbrush smothered in black shoe polish with a drop of spit added and the boots repeatedly rubbed in a circular movement until the leather took on a smooth appearance. Needless to say, this took many hours and any spare time we had would see us 'back to the boots', both pairs! The boots were then ready for polishing with a soft cloth over the index finger with more polish and spit to bring up the desired shine. I learnt this art well, so much so that later in my career I earned the reputation of having the 'best boots in the Regiment'. They were actually on one occasion used for a Recruiting Office Display when I later was stationed in Leicester. The Boys also taught me how to use a 'burnisher' for cleaning spurs and swords, which was to stand me in good stead up and until the Regiment went over to mechanisation.

Every Wednesday afternoon we would participate in sports or physical training and I was delighted when invited to join in the Regimental Boys Football Team to play The West Kents' Boys; so with the rest of the team I went to the Sports Stores to draw my football kit. They had no boots to fit me, the smallest size they had was seven and this was two sizes too big for me, but there was no alternative if I wanted to play, so I took them and endeavoured to give a good account of myself on the field, in spite of the boots. My effort went down well with the other Boys; I had, in fact broken the ice; I was accepted.

When there were no sporting activities we would go to the gymnasium for the afternoon, but if the weather permitted we would go for a 'run' into Hythe, a distance of five miles, rounded off by a dip on the sea; a welcome change from the camp environment.

The Boys soon took me into their confidences and taught me some 'tricks of the trade' whereby I could survive financially. One of these was running errands for the bandsmen at tea-breaks. This would entail going to The

Soldiers' Home, which was nearer to the Bandroom than the NAAFI and less crowded, to fetch tea and cakes for the men. Now the price of a mug of tea was sixpence but we purchased only threepence worth; then we'd rush back to the wash-house, top up from the hot water tap, filling the mug to the brim and repeat this until all the orders were completed. It used to make for a very hectic tea-break while it lasted, often leaving us no time for any tea ourselves, but we'd have made quite a profit! There were often complaints about the tea, but no-one ever fathomed out the dodge.

It wasn't long, seeing I had joined a Cavalry Regiment, that I had my first insight to horses. As I now had my canvas I went to the stables to help with 'mucking out'. I had never been close to a horse before, so the sight of these massive beasts I found somewhat frightening. On arrival at the stable I was amazed when the Corporal came to me and said, 'Take those two out for a drink,' pointing to the two horses in the stalls. I didn't protest, so with my heart in my mouth I ventured into the stalls, grabbed the head rope and caught the first horse, but how in God's name was I to get the other; it was beyond me! One of the Boys came to my rescue by giving me one of his that he was leading, so out I went with the two huge beasts, one on either side of me, to the trough, where they drank their fill: now, how do I get these two beasts away from the trough without getting trampled to death? I decided that if I backed, maybe they would too. I tried it and, lo and behold, they conformed! So off I went in the direction of the stables making sure they didn't crowd me or tread on my feet. Suddenly, something startled one of my horses and before I knew what was happening I was lifted off my feet hanging on the end of the rope in mid-air. I didn't want any more of that so I promptly let go of the ropes and guess what? The horses bolted! As there were some twenty or more other horses milling around this immediately started a miniature stampede. I ran for cover under the trough whilst they rounded them up. When I thought it was safe to come out I sneaked back to the stables only to be well and truly told off by the Corporal. But that was not the end of it. He straight away ordered me to take a wheelbarrow of dung to the manure heap. 'Yes, Sir,' says I, but I couldn't lift it to get the thing started. However, never say die! Once more and away I went, fifty yards downhill at the double, getting faster and faster. Realising it was getting the better of me, I aimed it at the dung heap and hoped for the best, but before I knew it, it had reached the heap, gave a nasty lurch and I was thrown headlong into the dung. Phew! That was it! I extricated myself and walked off in disgust, howling my eyes out.

Fortunately, I had been issued a second suit of canvas (designed for such occasions I should imagine) so I cleaned up and presented myself for breakfast and then to band practice. Later that evening I had the job of washing my stinking canvas from the early morning's episode. I managed to cadge a chunk of washing soap for the task, usually used for scrubbing the forms and tables and it worked a treat. Once they had dried, I then had to iron them by heating the iron on the fire – no mean task. That was my first lesson at dhobying and it wasn't to be the last.

At band practice the Bandmaster gave me a clarinet and set me a few tests to find out just how much I knew. I passed all the tests, which seemed to please him and made me feel that I had got off to a good start. Spike, by the way, seemed to be sailing through everything with fewer mishaps. We were both sent to the Boys' room to practice. We soon discovered the windows looked out on to the Riding School, so we passed the time of day watching the recruits going through their various stages of riding and jumping. This appealed to me more than my first encounter with the horses at 'mucking out' and whetted my appetite for the day when I too would be doing something similar at Riding School.

After a fortnight I was sent to the tailors to try on my new uniforms and as they fitted so I was ordered to parade with the band on Sunday for Church Parade. Both Spike and I spent all day Saturday preparing our kit for our very first Church Parade. On Sunday we presented ourselves in full Cavalry rig, breeches, putties and spurs, to a loud cheer from all the Bandsmen. After inspection we marched through the town for two miles to the Garrison Church. I'd had lots of marching practice at school but here, on my first adult parade, I found it difficult to match their strides and was greatly relieved when we arrived. I was almost in a state of collapse; the musical side had been easy. Having had a Church of England religious education at school I was well versed with the form of service, so when instructed to undertake choir duties, this I was well able to do. On returning to Barracks I noticed several civilian photographers busy taking photos of personnel. This was a memorable day for me so I decided to have a photograph taken, which I have to this day. The rest of the days were spent cleaning and preparing all my kit for the following days, and so to bed at 9.30pm.

Time was passing and I was getting into the swing of things, always remembering that soon I would be leaving these shores for foreign parts.

Friday, as nearly everyone knows was 'Pay Day' in the Army, so I gladly 'fell in' for my very first pay parade. When my name was called I proudly went forward, saluted, and stuck out my hand. I received sixpence to last me the week, or at least I thought I had, but there were others with different ideas. Before I could get out of the Pay Office the NCO in charge of Boys demanded threepence off me. 'For coal,' he said. 'You don't think we manage on what they allow us, do you.' I wasn't going to be as well off as I had first thought! Still, I was making quite a bit on the side. No wonder we fiddled!

Christmas arrived, my first in the Army, and I knew it wouldn't be like my Christmases at school. They were good, as the entire resident staff would go out of their way to make it the highlight of the year. There was always a trip, each year, by the whole school to the Circus at Olympia in London, eagerly looked forward to. Also, every child would receive a present off the enormous tree, in addition to gifts sent by our families, and in the Chapel which was beautifully decorated, we would have a Carol Service, to which all friends and relatives were invited. Weeks before Christmas, the huge communal Dining Hall would take on a completely different appearance as the lanterns and paper-chains slowly and inexorably took over, reaching perfection, so it seemed, on Christmas Eve.

That was all behind me as I proceeded home on leave. I was given four pounds to go with, putting me further into debt, but who worries about such things at Christmas? At least I didn't have to pay my fare as I was given travel warrants. Imagine the thrill when I alighted at Addlestone Station, my first time there since I was five years old and here I was dressed in my military uniform - a Boy Soldier! I marched through the town with my whip (part of the walking out dress) tucked under my arm. I can tell you I turned a few eyes. During the ten days leave period I met lots of old school chums, themselves on leave from their various regiments, who also lived with foster parents in or around Addlestone. Whilst wandering around the shops my eye caught sight of a live goose in the butcher's window. I thought that would make a nice surprise for Mum and Dad so I popped in and purchased it. I hadn't thought very much about how I was going to get it home until it was placed under my arm. I must have looked a comical sight with this huge goose struggling for its' freedom and me, in military uniform, endeavouring to keep it within my grasp. Folk were amused as I went on my way and eventually I arrived home to the delight of my folks. Dad relieved me of the goose and disappeared into the shed whilst Mum hugged and kissed me. My efforts had been well rewarded when Mum produced it on the table on Christmas Day. Lots of friends visited us while I was home. Although it had been totally different to my previous Christmases, it had certainly been a memorable one and all too soon I had to entrain for Shorncliffe and back to barrack life once again. By now, I had become used to travelling on my own.

Back at the Barracks as I was only attached to the 15th/ 19th Hussars I did not start Riding School but carried out stable duties only. The men had pity on me after my first experience with horses and just gave me cleaning jobs to do. I soon got the upper hand of a wheelbarrow full of muck and began to love this working with horses and, of course, lost my fear of them.

The 'BOY' as Duty Trumpeter with Regimental Policeman Ben Beanland. He who bet me I wouldn't blow dismount at the Married Quarters.

CHAPTER 3

Overseas Service

Time was passing fast and now, as we got nearer our sailing date of April 7th 1935, things began to happen.

We were issued our Tropical Kit, such as Drill Uniforms, Topees and a Pugree. This was a long scarf-like piece of material, which was wrapped round and round the Topee in such a way so as to give one protection from the hot sun. I soon mastered this art and, again, as in the case of my S.D. Uniform, all my uniform was made to measure so these and various other items set me back a further five pounds, and so my debt kept growing. Then came embarkation leave - two weeks of it. I was glad to be going home again and the whole two weeks was spent in a hectic round of farewells. This spell home was the last time I saw my folks for many along year. By the way, the Army had given me a further five pounds for this latest leave and I was convinced by now that by the time I reached Egypt my debt to the Army would be as big as the National Debt!

As my Army equipment swelled to a gigantic size, I began to wonder how I was going to travel halfway round the world with it. First, there was the Universal Kitbag, that was the one almost as big as me; then there was the Sea Kitbag, not quite so tall but when filled, much heavier; plus a big pack, full, to carry on my back; a Mess Tin and water bottle over my shoulder and a haversack over the other. However, I dare say I would make it, just as other youngsters had done before me!

During my temporary attachment to the 15th/19th Hussars men had come from various walks of life in Civvy Street to Shorncliffe for service overseas and so it was that on the morning of April 7th, a total of fifty men and five Boys (including Spike and me) entrained for Southampton en route to join the 8th Hussars in Egypt. We embarked on HMS Devonshire along with others and prepared to leave for the Middle East and beyond. Each man drew a hammock and was allotted a mess deck where at night we were to sleep.

The weather didn't look too promising when we set sail at 2pm. As we progressed down the Solent I began to feel something was happening to my stomach, which steadily worsened as we pressed on towards the open sea.

We were still in sight of land when we had a boat drill. I, with my lifejacket round my neck, lined up with the rest on the port side from which the wind was blowing. Suddenly, a massive wave broke over the side and knocked me into the 'scuppers'. Someone picked me up and helped me back into line. Now I was not only sick but also soaking wet and feeling very sorry for myself. Once we were dismissed I made a beeline for the rails where I emptied out.

Feeling bloody awful, I made my way very unsteadily down to the Mess Deck where I hoped to get dried out and warm. It was now suppertime but all I could manage was a steaming hot mug of cocoa and then prepared for bed. This meant rigging up my hammock, which I did, after a fashion, and attempted to clamber in, which was easier said than done. After several abortive attempts, I eventually nestled down to sleep but the sight of a hundred hammocks all swinging to and fro in unison and the creaking of the ropes was too much for me. It sent me racing again to the washroom. On arrival there, I was horrified to find every basin was in use by other personnel in a far worse state than I. It was a case of getting in where and when I could!

Once my stomach had settled I again thought of sleep but just couldn't be bothered with applying the knack of getting into a hammock so I took the easy way out and settled on a Mess Deck table. Snatches of sleep was all that I could get what with the violent rolling of the ship, at times almost throwing me off the table, and my upset stomach.

Reveille was sounded at 6am and the ship was a hive of activity with everyone up for one reason or another and the sea still 'blowing it's top'. As the smell of bacon and eggs wafted through the air, my stomach gave a heave and it was back to the washroom. This time I secured a basin, which I refused to leave till the ship docked at Gibraltar – a wise decision as it turned out, because the weather conditions were atrocious as we went through the Bay of Biscay. Some of my pals, who by now had got their sea-legs, were to bring me all sorts of delicacies, such as tripe and onions and pork and beans – little wonder I never lifted my head out of that basin until Gibraltar was reached!

Three or four days later the seas subsided and we sailed into Gibraltar in calm waters. For me, everything took on a new life as I washed and cleaned myself. I was feeling great as I went up on deck for the first time since our initial boat-drill. The ship was still; the sun shining and the difference in temperature was very noticeable. The natives in their bum-boats were swarming all around the ship, hoping to rook the gullible soldiers with bargains and souvenirs. The soldiers gave as good as they got from the safety of the ship; all sorts of things were thrown overboard onto the bum-boats. I ate a hearty meal and all-in-all was feeling on top of the world when we pulled out from Gibraltar.

The rest of the trip was just a cruise. Some of the ship's crew and some old soldiers who had been through it all before produced the Crown and Anchor Boards; there was tombola on the upper deck and a band was playing on the Officer's Deck. Several groups were playing cards, in fact, the lower deck was transformed into a Casino. My part in all this was to watch out for any officer approaching the Mess Deck and warn the Crown and Anchor operators. For this I was given ten shillings (50p). I was beginning to like this trip!

Apart from those previously mentioned, there were other entertainments on board such as concerts, shipboard sports, films and, on one occasion, a concert with the soldiers being the 'stars' themselves. All too soon we reached Malta and here the men were allowed ashore. Not so us boys. Nevertheless, we had lots to amuse us; chief of all was soaking up the sun for which we suffered later. Then there were the usual bum-boats from which we made some purchases. With everyone back on board we were again on the move, this time for Alexandria, Egypt.

On the second day out of Malta I won the ship's sweep on how many miles the ship would travel in twenty-four hours. With this cash prize, plus my ten shillings a day from the

Crown and Anchor operators, I had a tidy sum when we reached Alex, in spite of the fact that I had lost a bet I attempted on the 'Boards'. We all changed our sterling into Egyptian money, one hundred piastres or 'akkers' as we called them, to the pound, before we disembarked. After this the Medical Officer gave us a lecture on the dangers of disease in Egypt and told us in no uncertain terms how dirty and disease-ridden were the places we were going to. We anchored in the harbour overnight, ready to disembark in the morning.

Alexandria Harbour was, and is, a very busy place. I stayed up on deck late into the night watching the comings and goings of all sorts of craft; merchant ships, battleships and some ships I couldn't begin to put a name to. The night was as one would read about in books. The air was warm with sounds floating across the harbour intermingled with native music (which to me sounded all very weird), making a cacophony of sounds which could not be separated. A myriad of lights of all colours were twinkling and swinging in the breeze. The few natives I could see appeared to be dressed in nightshirts; this mode of dress, I know now, was the Egyptian national dress called a 'jalabhi'. I didn't sleep at all that night; I was too excited. I just packed my kit and awaited disembarkation.

At 8.30am the troops started to disembark and while I awaited my turn I stood and surveyed the scene. The early morning sounds were quite different from those of the night before. The Mullahs were all calling the population to prayer from the minarets of the city. The view over Alexandria was something I had never imagined but I was to see quite a lot of it in the future. Our draft went ashore about 11am. The train which was to take us to Cairo pulled up beside the ship so it was easy going with all my kit to get aboard.

The Egyptian trains were quite primitive compared to those of England. The all-wooden seats left much to be desired, were dirty and thoroughly uncomfortable and, of course, there were no toilet facilities which on a long journey was, to say the least, inconvenient. This was not a troop train but we did have reserved carriages so we had to travel with the natives and on seeing them at close quarters, I was not over-impressed. For instance, the women who all wore black dresses with veils over their faces, appeared dirty and smelt of garlic. Those who were carrying children in their arms thought nothing of exposing breasts to feed them; they ignored the flies that swarmed all over them which rather horrified me. The men, who needed to, just urinated outside the door; their clothes were creased, stained and patched and their headdress, called a 'tarbrush' or fez, was in a similar state. Altogether to me they looked a pretty scruffy lot.

The journey was educational. I saw sights that dated back to biblical times as we passed through countryside which seemed to have stood still for thousands of years. I saw camels driving waterwheels, blindfolded donkeys and sometimes oxen doing the same job. We passed Egyptians riding small donkeys with their legs almost touching the ground, flapping from side to side. At times we would see natives kneeling in prayer; dirty kids carrying heavy loads on their heads and women in black carrying pitchers on their heads with babies strung to their backs. We passed Mosques with minarets and small, antiquated country stations the names of which were written in Arabic and when called out sounded to me rather like 'gobbledegook'.

Whenever the train stopped at any official stops the train would be invaded by hawkers trying to sell their wares of lemonade, eggs and bread, or some other horrible looking Egyptian food like chapattis filled with rice and curry. These would be very heavily spiced judging by the scent that wafted over the air. Small children would be among them, trying to sell what they called souvenirs.

The train travelled through a variety of countryside as we sped for Cairo. We passed miles of plantations of cotton, rice and other cereals all being irrigated by various means. One system which intrigued me greatly was carried out by a man sitting beside what appeared to be a huge cylinder, turning a handle attached to same, which turned the cylinder, with water pouring out of one end into an irrigation ditch which appeared to encircle the plantation. This way they would water their crops.

We had quite an insight into their wildlife too from the train; apparently it was quite commonplace for myriads of storks and cranes to be seen standing about, watching the rest of the world go by.

I got the impression too that children made up a large part of the population, so many would we see playing in the sand or pushing home-made carts and prams, always in a dirty condition and surrounded by flies, which didn't seem to bother them one bit. All in all, my first train journey through Egypt had been quite an eye-opener.

It was mid-afternoon when we arrived at Cairo, very hot and dusty. The people milling around the station were representative of about every nation on earth. Everywhere was hustle and bustle and a little confusing for me, so it was with relief when our draft was led from the station to the Regimental Bus by a sergeant sent to pick us up. I was confused even further as we drove through the crowded streets on the right side of the street. There were donkey carts and camel trains all trying to make their way through the traffic; noisy trams clanging their bells with people hanging all over them and kids getting on and off just when they pleased. Horse-drawn carriages or gharries, as they were called, were much in evidence, as the driver picked his way through the conglomeration of traffic. Beside the roadside were open-fronted bars where the natives sat smoking hubbly-bubblys (or *hookahs*) and from where very loud Egyptian music came as if to compete with the noise of the traffic. Vendors were shouting their wares; people rushing hither and thither, and in a second one could see the world go by and

THE BAND MARCHING INTO ALEX C. OF A. 1936

nearly all, it seemed, were covered in flies and dust. The stench that pervaded the air was offensive to the nostrils to say the least.

We eventually arrived at our destination via the village of Abbassia, from which the Barracks got it's name. As we alighted from the Regimental Bus I noticed it was painted in old gold and emerald; these were our regimental colours.

So this was the end of the journey which had taken just over three weeks and brought me to Egypt on the threshold of my career.

My address for the next few years was to be:

554766 Boy R. Napier
8th K.R.I. Hussars,
Main Barracks,
Abbassia, Cairo, Egypt.

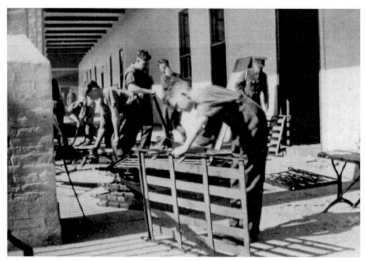

WEDNESDAY – DE-BUGGING.

ON DUTY AT HELIOPOLIS RACES

CHAPTER 4

Egypt

On arrival at Main Barracks we were met by the Regimental Sergeant Major (RSM), a representative from each Squadron and the Band Corporal, by the Guardroom at the entrance of the Barracks. The RSM welcomed us to the regiment with a short speech of welcome and then we were all dispatched to our appropriate squadrons whilst us Boys were taken to the Band Quarters and then on to The Boys Room on the second floor of a two storey barrack block. We were allotted our beds, then, equipped with our own cutlery and mug and then shown to the Dining Hall which was some thirty yards from the Cookhouse where we collected our food. Returning to the Dining Hall here could be hazardous; nobody had warned us of the kitehawks. Apparently, these birds of prey lay in wait for the unsuspecting to swoop down on them and snatch the food from off their plates and fly off with it. The strange thing about these birds was that should you be aware and be prepared for them, they would not attack. As I was the last to be served, and had seen what was going on, I made the Dining Hall without mishap, but very scared. The rest of the day was spent being introduced to everyone and getting acquainted and sorting out our kit. For this, we were issued with a locker and were shown how to pack our kit into it, in a set pattern. So ended an eventful day.

The following day dawned with the sounds of Reveille at 5.30am and the first day much as my first day with the 15th/19th Hussars with parades of introduction, kit inspections and cleaning. My uniform issued at Shorncliffe had to be discarded (which had cost me £5) because it was of a different shade to that of the 8th Hussars. A further two suits of the correct shade were tailored for me at the coast of £3.50, thus swelling my existing debt. The cap I purchased for seven and sixpence was also of no use in the 8th Hussars, theirs being of a 'superfine' quality. A new cap set me back a further 35 akkers – there was no end to it!

Once they had our uniforms sorted out we had to report to the Medical Centre for inoculations against the endemic diseases of Egypt and a further lecture from the MO on the perils of VD – how to avoid it – and the importance of personal hygiene, coupled with a warning about food and drink purchased from the natives.

With that over, we were taken on a tour of the Barracks. We saw the classrooms where we would continue our education; then on to the Slade Sportsground and Club. This was the main Sports Centre of the Garrison. We came next to the NAAFI, via the tennis courts, and finally to the Parade Ground in the centre of which was a boxing ring. I knew I was going to enjoy it here, in spite of the oppressive heat, which would take some getting used to.

We, the draft, settled down into the regimental routine. Within a week I had been issued with a trumpet. Remembering what the MO had told me on my enlistment, I explained to the Trumpet Major why I should not play the trumpet. He grinned and said

'You try, and if you get into trouble, we'll take you to our MO and if he excuses you from blowing a trumpet, you'll be excused.' He continued, 'until then, blow on, my son.'

Hence, I became a trumpeter along with the rest of the band.

Regimental routines are pretty well the same throughout the army, except for a few minor variations. In hot climates such as we were in, Reveille would be earlier, working through to lunch. The rest of the day was usually spent on the sports field, although the men had a choice of 'in bed or out of barracks'. This did not apply to Boys. We had to be playing sport or cleaning our kit. This was especially beneficial to me as, in view of my small stature, I had intended at all cost to develop it, so I took to sport in a big way.

Within weeks of my arrival I was on my first 'mounted parade'. This was in June 1935, when King George V of England celebrated his Silver Jubilee. My regiment, along with others in the Garrison, were to take part in a Jubilee Parade at Gezira Sporting Club in Cairo. I was put on a 'crash course' for this, in riding which taught me the rudiments of riding on a very docile horse. This was the thrill of my life. I was quick to learn how to sit on a horse properly and keep my balance whilst the horse started to trot, everything went wrong. I began to lose my equilibrium – first a gradual slip to the right, then a slip to the left - with each pace of the horse until I eventually lost control altogether and just gently slipped out of the saddle.

'Who told you to dismount?' my instructor shouted. 'Collect your horse and re-mount!'

It took me some time and several miles of running before both the horse and I were under complete control. I had a lot to learn and I knew I had to learn quickly. As 'trotting' didn't come into my present course, I carried on gripping like hell with my knees, whilst learning to control my horse without hands.

Then I had to learn to play the clarinet at the same time. I spent hours under instruction doing just that. There was a snag however; I couldn't reach the saddle or get my foot in the stirrup as was required by the Drill Orders, so it was decided that when the order to 'Mount' was given, I was to get on my horse as best as I could. Provided no horse shied or panicked on the Day, I reckoned and so did my instructor that I should get by. Meanwhile, I continued with my education, band practice, learning the various trumpet calls, attending to my kit for the parade, including my riding instruction every evening. Is it any wonder I retired to bed at 9.30pm exhausted!

Reveille was early on Jubilee Day. I was very excited to be participating in my first 'Mounted Parade'. After a good breakfast the band paraded outside the Bandroom for inspection, then we marched to the Stables to take charge of our horses. These horses were selected principally because they were known to be quiet and would not adversely react to hearing musical instruments being blown into their ears. We bridled and saddled them before being finally inspected, then we mounted and proceeded 'at the walk' to the Regimental Parade Ground. Here we joined the regiment already formed into squadrons for the final inspection before proceeding en route for the Parade proper. At 9 a.m. we marched through Cairo to the Gazira Sports Club. There we met up with the King's Dragoon Guards and formed a massed band. The Parade 'fell in' and were inspected by the GOC British Troops, Egypt who, with the High Commissioner, 'took the salute' at the 'march past'; during which time the band played for the Inspection, the 'walk past' and the 'trot past'. The whole parade went without a hitch; my horse had been wonderful and I had come through with flying colours. Certainly, a day for me to remember. It was 2.30pm before we returned to barracks, to be dismissed to divest ourselves of our best uniforms (used in the parade) and also our instruments; then back to the Stables to attend to the horses. This involved grooming them, cleaning the saddle and, in general, leaving the Stables spick and span as we had found them. The band did not have their own horses.

In spite of giving a good account of myself on parade, my riding lessons continued along with the others. The Boys had a special Boys Course. We would be taken out to the desert on the north side of the Stables where the instructor would put us through our paces. One lad, nicknamed 'Hitler' because of the physical likeness, never seemed able to hold his horse 'at the canter', so at the end of the session when we were allowed to canter, Hitler's horse would get the bit between it's teeth and bolt in a cloud of dust, with Hitler heard shouting:

'Whoa! WHOA!'

Needless to say, he was always back at the Stables first.

Apart from riding, music and normal duties, sport was a major feature of life in the Middle East. In the Cairo area there were eight different regiments and each had its complement of Boys. The Infantry regiments had twenty whilst the Cavalry had only eleven and the Artillery had about six Trumpeters. In football, cricket, shooting and other eleven-men team events, there was a Boys League, so there was always plenty of sport available. In order that the Artillery Boys could take part they amalgamated with the 8th Hussars and always provided a combined team.

Summers in Cairo were really hot and sticky, so I sought out the swimming pool whenever possible. Within the barracks we had a very small bath which was called 'The Chatti', where I was to be found at every available opportunity. Later the Army built a full-sized swimming pool in the Garrison. It had all the facilities of an Olympic Pool and was named ALI Friend, after the Brigadier of Cavalry. Swimming training was taken very seriously indeed, now that the Army no longer needed to share the civilian swimming pools at Heliopolis and Ezbekieh. Frequent competitions and swimming galas were held, which greatly improved performance.

I was now becoming quite a proficient trumpeter, good enough to commence 'Trumpet Guards'. At first I would go on guard with one of the bandsmen as a supernumerary. After three of these I was considered good enough to mount guard on my own and was officially listed on the Guard Roll. The duties of the 'Duty Trumpeter' would entail sounding a variety of calls throughout the day, such as Reveille (5.30am), Breakfast, Stables, Mail, Defaulters, Orderly Sergeants,

Officers' Mess, Dinner, First Post, Last Post, Lights Out and any calls requested by the RSM. When the regiment was mounted I had to know calls appertaining to mounted drills i.e. mount, dismount, walk-march, trot, charge, wheels, etc.

In the late summer of '35 I was put on my first trumpet guard duty for a twenty-four hour period commencing at 6pm. We would mount guard along with the other guards then report to the guardroom which was to be our base for the period of duty. After sounding 'lights out' we could then sleep in the guardroom, although on call. At 5am I was called by the sentry, giving me time to wash, clean up and get a mug of 'gunfire' (the first mug of tea of the day) so that my lips and mouth were in good order to blow 'reveille'. This was the longest and the most difficult of the entire trumpeter's repertoire. The duty policeman was called at the same time and on this particular morning it was Lance Corporal Ben Beanland, who was a bit of a practical joker, which I was to find out to my peril. Just prior to blowing Reveille he said to me 'Tich, I bet you ten akkers you won't go over to Married Quarters and blow 'dismount'. The bet was too good to miss, so for ten akkers, after a bit of thought, I marched over to the Married Quarters and blew the regimental call and followed it with 'dismount'.

I was about to walk away when a voice yelled out from the balcony of the Married Quarters.

'Trumpeter, what the hell do you think you are playing at?'

Then he shouted across to the guardroom.

'Policeman, when this boy has blown Reveille, put him in the guardroom.'

It was the RSM. I went back to the grinning cop who waited for me to blow reveille. He gave me the ten akkers and promptly marched me to the jail. For that dastardly crime I received seven days 'defaulters' (commonly known as 'jankers'), which denied me any free time and turned out to be a very hard working week indeed. I certainly resisted any future urge to do that again, for any amount of money!

By now I was participating in and enjoying a variety of sports. I had been selected for the boys' cricket team just to make up the number, but swimming was a different matter. It was getting a hold on me, especially as I was now being coached by a member of the regimental swimming team who held the 220 and 440 yards freestyle records and who also played for the Army water polo team. I also progressed to diving; my ability at this was to be proven later.

The boys were occasionally allowed to the garrison cinema, but only on Saturday afternoons, along with the schoolchildren. In the summer it was held in the open air. Whilst on Boys' Service, I could get in for half-price so it was an opportunity not to be missed. It was on one of these occasions that I spoke to a girl for the first time. Her name was Muriel and she lived in Married Quarters with her parents at the Remount Depot, within the Garrison, about one and a half miles away.

After dating her a few times at the cinema, I arranged to visit her at home. Before setting out, I prepared my kit for inspection and also arranged with the other Boy that should anyone want me they were to say I was in the Canteen. It was a beautiful summer's evening that we spent in her garden. Muriel and I, just chatting away the hours, when I heard in the distance a bugler sounding the quarter hour call. I looked at my watch and to my dismay saw the time was 9.15pm. I had to be in bed at 9.30pm, so I said a hurried goodnight and fled. I realised I had about ten minutes to get back to barracks and in bed before the duty NCO came round to check. Off I set at a pretty good pace, I ran and ran and shot past the guardroom just as the duty trumpeter was coming out to sound the first post at 9.30. I asked him, 'wait one minute' and rushed on. Up to the band block, down a small corridor, past the duty NCO's bunk, then in to the boys' room. I jumped into bed fully dressed, shoes and all and lay there panting. I heard the bunk door open and footsteps heading our way. Our door opened and a stern voice said, 'Who the hell has just flown past my door as though the bats of hell were after him?'

Nobody spoke. I lay motionless but still panting. He commenced to check the kits and on approaching my bed he paused, ripping off my bedding to reveal me fully dressed.

'All right Napier,' he said, 'up you get.'

I knew I was in trouble.

'I'll see you in the morning,' he said, and off he went, leaving me standing. I got 10 days extra fatigues for that little episode...

I had by now become accustomed to the band routine and the wide variety of musical programmes: fortnightly band concerts on the square in summer and at the Slade Club in winter; weekly programmes at our officers mess on Tuesdays and the RHA officers mess on Wednesdays; church parades on Sundays and, if we were duty band, any funerals that might occur. For all these programmes there would be intensive practice sessions, which I enjoyed tremendously.

But the events I looked forward to most were the attendances at the racecourses at Gazira and Heliopolis. Not only was it an opportunity to have a little flutter, which was permitted (by kind permission of the Bandmaster) but these were 'paid engagements'. There were others too, such as attendances at garden parties, sports events at private schools and at gymkhanas. The money for these engagements was paid out on a 'shares basis' (i.e. the band fund would receive 15 shares, the Bandmaster 10 shares, then down the scale until we Boys got a 'boy's share', paid out monthly). Should any bandsman require an urgent sub, it was usually forthcoming after applying personally to the Bandmaster. In addition to these payments were the 'perks' that went with the job, and I still recall the occasion we were engaged to play at a girls' convent school in Abbassia at their annual sports and physical training display.

It was a very hot day so the nuns provided us with liquid refreshment in the form of iced beer. This was placed in a five foot galvanised bath, filled with ice and set down beside the drummer. During the afternoon, the drummer observed that a nun would creep up to the bath, remove as many bottles as she could carry and then disappear. This ritual was repeated until finally, the bath became completely empty. At tea break, the nuns waited on us, and it became apparent that some of them had lost their normal composure and were, to say the least, decidedly 'merry'. It goes without saying that this was not their usual habit! Nevertheless, a good time was had by all and it was a memorable day.

CHAPTER 5

The end of an era

Sad news was going around that the Regiment was to lose its horses and become mechanised. This would indeed be a great loss to those of us who had learned to live with the great hairy beasts; it would mean a whole new way of life, in fact. I had done a short 'boy's course' on riding and loved every minute of it – except in the initial stages when I frequently became unseated! Because I couldn't carry out the normal mounting drill because of my size, I was allowed to make my own way up on command. The orders went like this:

"Stand to your horses... Prepare to mount... Mount! ...... Napier, get up!"

Such was the humour among cavalrymen, yes, even Sergeant Majors! In the event of mechanisation, this would all be lost.

In spite of my size, I was growing up fast! I was often sent on errands for the older men and on one occasion I had to go to the Sergeants' Mess with a message for the band sergeant. He liked his beer and we Boys often suffered because of it. Having rung the bell, I waited around and noticed a glass of beer sitting unattended on a table. I made sure nobody was looking, then I sneaked up to it and took a long drink – it was foul – and I took an instant dislike to it. Needless to say it held no future attraction for me. Hours later, having delivered my message to the band sergeant, I had a severe attack of colic which was to set me on a teetotalers' course for many a year.

I mentioned earlier that boys from my school were drafted into every regiment of the British Army and on occasions I would meet some of them during sporting activities. I mention one in particular who had been in the Seaforth Highlanders for three years. When I saw him and chatted to him, to my surprise he spoke in a broad Scottish accent. I couldn't believe my ears, and I was in for another surprise – they beat us 4 – 1 on the football field.

Winter was coming on, but in Egypt, the temperatures do not fall to freezing, although in comparison to the summer months, the days and nights were cold. So we discarded our Khaki Drill and reverted to 'SD' as worn in UK, which was normal procedure in Egypt.

It was also the boxing season and I was invited to 'have a go' ... and like an idiot I said 'yes', not knowing what I was letting myself in for. I was soon to learn. So started a new sport for me! As no other boys had volunteered, I was on my own. About this time the various boxing competitions had started, leading up to the Middle East Championships, so my training began in earnest. The band corporal was regimental welterweight champ and another bandsman was the light-weight champ, so these two took me under their wings and taught me the noble art of self-defence. They knocked me about a bit, but said it was only 'to teach me to defend myself'. Eventually I was good enough, they thought, to enter for the Boys' Championships. Boys' weights in the Army differed from Mens' weights in that they commenced with Gnat weight, then on to Mosquito weight, followed by Fly weight and so on up to Boys' heavy. After weeks of sparring, running, shadow boxing and general training, the time came for the 'weigh-in' at the Garrison Gym. A call for 'Mosquitoes' went up and six of us Boys stepped forward. They were all weighed and checked correct. Then I got on to the scales, but nothing happened, several ounces were removed and there was a flicker, two more ounces and that was it – I was too light for the Mosquitoes. So on my behalf a challenge was sent out for any Gnatweight to take me on. There were 'no takers' – my arm was raised there and then I was declared 'Gnatweight champion of all Egypt' amid cheers and roars of laughter.

The story did not end there, due mainly to my own foolishness. The Sgt Major PT called me over and told me I would have to wait another year, unless... 'You would like to take a chance and go into the draw with the Mosquitoes'. Well, I hadn't trained hard for nothing, so like an idiot I agreed, amid much applause from the assembled boxers. Into the hat went my name and as you may have guessed, I was drawn to fight the biggest boy of the weight – an Irish guardsman, Boy Hughes. Training intensified, with long runs into the desert north of the barracks and on into Old Cairo, known as 'The Dead City'.

This old city was completely derelict with just some of the Mosques preserved and in some cases still in use. We went into one which we were told by the Mufti was nearly two thousand years old. He allowed us to look around, after leaving our shoes outside, and barefooted we wandered around full of wonder that this had in fact been built in

Biblical times and was still in a perfect state of preservation. He drew our attention to the window above the door. All I could see was a stained glass window with a small lizard on it and this was not surprising, as lizards were very prevalent and seen almost anywhere in Egypt. Then he said, 'look closer'. On further inspection I perceived that the lizard was encased in the window. It had become accidentally entombed there when the Mosque had been built ... two thousand years ago.

Also in this old city was an ancient narrow-gauge railway with its original engine which used to chug to and fro hauling sand and granite to various building companies. We quite often hitched a lift.

It was early November (I'd just celebrated my sixteenth birthday) when the boxing championships were due to start, so I was sent to the sports store to draw a regimental singlet, (green and gold). If the heavyweight had been just in front of me, he would have got that singlet; there was only one size! Far too big! When I put it on, the open neckline was in my shorts; it came down well below my knees and the straps kept slipping off my shoulders. What a state! However, in the changing room my seconds came to my rescue... but they came up with a brilliant idea which was to cause me much trouble. They tied four knots in the straps which stopped them slipping; the green stripe was still visible and now the bottom of the singlet was no longer coming out of the legs of my shorts.

At the first bell my opponent came out for the kill. He must have overlooked the fact that he was up against the 'Gnat Weight Champion', who knew how to duck and dodge out of trouble, for he had a job to pin me down. But not for long; he soon got the measure, as I ducked in under his left to thump him on the kneecap or occasionally catch him on the chest, but all the while he was thumping hell out of me. When the bell sounded for the end of the first round, my seconds were full of encouragement.

'You've got him Tich,' they said. 'He's groggy; he doesn't know what day it is.'

To be honest, neither did I, but I wasn't going to tell them.

Again the bell summoned us out and away we went; he thumping me and I thumping fresh air. Then he caught on. He persisted with either a left or right hook, aiming at the knots standing up beside my ears, and didn't it hurt! This would do all the damage needed to put me out of action he must have thought as he hammered away. I was feeling I had had enough when, mercifully for me, the bell called a halt to the second round. I told my seconds about the knots and showed them my very bruised ears. With seconds only to work in, he snipped off the offending knots and I was out for the last and final round. I managed to use my superior speed to keep out of trouble; in fact, at these times he didn't know where I was as I darted in to bash him anywhere I could reach and then retreat behind the corner post. Catastrophe! Just before the bell rung to conclude the match. The knots on my singlet had worked loose, baring my chest as it fell down below my waist. I think I nearly knocked out my opponent with laughter when the final bell went and I was saved for another day. I got the biggest cheer of the night (probably for the comedy I had put on) and was congratulated. I didn't win... but I did come second! I was chaired back to the dressing room where my wounds were treated and, looking like the proverbial broken doll, I stayed to watch the other contests.

I retired to bed very sore, with a swollen nose, black eyes and, of course, thick ears. Came the morning and business as usual. I was excused band practice and put to repairing musical scores. At break time I returned my tattered singlet to the Stores. You're not going to believe this, but it's true. The Storeman nearly had a fit when he saw the condition of it. He straightway pulled out a form, which being completed meant I had to pay for it. I protested but, as he pointed out, it was not fair wear and tear but wilful damage. So my first boxing lesson had been very expensive, both physically and financially.

About this time, Freddie Brooker enlisted as a band Boy. He was the son of an airman from RAF Heliopolis. He joined us in order that he could play Rink Hockey for the Regiment, which he did to great effect. Thanks to the Band President, Major Tug Watson, Rink Hockey flourished within the Regiment. We were able to produce two teams to enter the Cairo Leagues. The first team, 'The Crossbelts' finished top of 'A' League, and the second team 'The Iron Horse' of which I was a reserve, was runner-up in the 'B' League. There were several good roller skating rinks in Cairo with two or three in Alexandria. I was now granted permission to go to these rinks for the purpose of practice with The Iron Horse Team.

There were other activities going on during the latter part of '35.

Orders had come through that the 8th Hussars were to be turned into a Light Car Reconnaissance Regiment, so after two hundred and forty years the Regiment's role was to change from that of a Cavalry Regiment to an Armoured Regiment. We were to be equipped with 15-hundredweight Ford V8 pick-ups with a Vickers Berthier machine gun mounted in the front. The value of such a formation as the Mechanised Cavalry Regiment in certain circumstances was to be obvious – swift-moving and silent with great fire power, it could be used for reconnaissance, for exploitation of success, for holding ground or for an independent mission. Mechanisation involved retraining throughout the entire Regiment. This entailed sending small groups of men on various courses of instruction to the 11th Hussars at Helmeih, who in their turn would train the Regiment for it's future role.

November 11th, Armistice Day, was the date set for the last Mounted Parade of the 8th K.R.I. Hussars to be held in the desert at Coombe Hill. The three Sabre Squadrons with the mounted band were on parade. It was a sad magnificent sight as the GOC made his final inspection, after which the Regiment trotted past, wheeled and then galloped past for the last time.

An equally sad occasion was on November 21st, when our horses were handed over to the Royal Dragoons who were on their way to England from India. So ended an era which included many famous Battle Honours. The most famous of these was 'The Charge of the Light Brigade Balaklava' in which the 8th Hussars played a prominent part.

THE BAND BOYS – EGYPT 1937.

CHAPTER 6

Trainee Bandsman

We were now a mechanised unit and one of the advantages we derived from this fact was that Reveille was put back to 6.30a.m. One thing the troops did not like was that early morning physical training was made compulsory.

The musical programme was going on as usual and I was now promoted from third to second clarinet. Concerts were still going on at the Slade Club and on the Square. Here, I would like to give you an insight into how these concerts were put together. Notices would be sent round to all regiments in the Cairo area inviting anybody who thought they may have some talent to contact our Bandmaster for an audition. This way we found some really first class performers. One of these was a Sergeant Joseph McLaughlin of the Irish Guards who was an excellent tenor and who later was to become world famous as 'The Irish Tenor', Joseph Lock.

At one of these auditions, a Private of the Royal Tank Regiment turned up and when interviewed said 'I'm a ventriloquist but I don't have a dummy.'

'Give us a sample of what you can do,' requested the Bandmaster, which he did to good effect. 'Very good,' said the Bandmaster 'but what do we do about a dummy?' He glanced around the bandsmen allowing his eyes to dwell on me and his face eased into a smile.

'Oh no!' I said.

'Oh yes! said the Bandmaster.

So it was I who was to act as his dummy. I didn't fancy the idea but, as someone once said, 'Ours is not to reason why', so rehearsals were carried on in the arts of ventriloquism. I was fitted out with a school cap, blazer and shorts and, of course, a regimental scarf. I soon learnt how to open and close my mouth without making sound, co-ordinating with my master's voice; I felt like a proper Charlie and, no doubt, looked like one, but if it got a laugh, it was O.K. by me. On the night of the concert, when the curtains went up, I was seated next to my master feeling pretty stupid. Wisecracks were reverberating around the hall; the men were enjoying it and, in fact, the act went down very well. It had certainly been a novelty, the first of its kind in my time. We rounded off the act with me playing a solo on the Ocarina of 'Me and My Girl' followed by loud applause. So ended my stage career! There were more serious activities afoot.

Christmas was fast approaching and preparations were getting under way for the festivities. Meanwhile, the duty troops were getting on with mechanisation and on December 18th, 1935, 'C' Squadron, who were now fully mechanised, set forth for the Western Desert to join up with the newly formed Mobile Force, based in Mersa Matruh. This was necessary because the Italians were sabre-rattling in Tunisia and also in Abyssinia. The Regiment was going to be rather depleted over Christmas. The Band provided three dance bands at various places around Cairo and the Boys had to shift all the heavy gear to and from these venues.

A day in a Boy's life was, to say the least, a hectic one: when for instance the band was playing at the Officers' Mess or anywhere else, they would have to carry all the drum kit, the stands and all the heavy kit over to the site, set it up and at the conclusion of the programme during which they had been playing, they would have to get it all back again. This on top of a full day's normal duties, and when the Dance Band were on an evening engagement, they would have to hang about until midnight. If it was any later than that then we would have to clear it all away in the morning.

The boys were now having to do square bashing, whilst the men were involved in driving instruction. This rather disrupted the band's normal routine.

Mechanisation had it's funny side if you used your imagination. Can you imagine a regiment full of horse soldiers one day, and the next all drivers and not a single driving licence between them.

The Barrack square was used as a car park with the cars parked around the sides. I stood and watched one morning when a squadron was carrying out 'First Parade'. This is a drill movement and is carried out thus: on the command 'Stand to your cars', the crew of four would stand in line in front of their cars facing the front; the next order 'Start Up', the driver would run to his cab and start up looking every bit like a car racing circuit. The rest of the crew would turn about to face the car, which was just as well as many of the cars had been left in gear from the previous night's parking. As a result, some cars lurched backwards through the privet hedge which surrounded the square whilst others leapt forward, scattering the crews standing out in front. The chaos was soon brought under control and there were no reports of casualties, but these hazards must have been foreseen in the early stages by the Powers That Be, otherwise why should they make the crew turn round and face the car and be prepared to jump for their lives at the press of a button.

1935 faded into history, but not before mention is made of the fact that the band won the Tent Pitching Competition. The New Year was welcomed in with the traditional celebration with high hopes of more competition successes, with my assistance I very much hoped.

The change-over from horses to vehicles was in full swing with 'C' Squadron already mechanised and part of the Mobile Defence Force at Mersa Matruh. There they were to spend Christmas among the dust storms of the desert; not the snow-covered scenes of a traditional Yuletide in England! Neither were they to have their traditional Christmas dinner it seemed for a while. The turkeys dispatched by the Regiment from Abbassia to 'C' Squadron at Mersa Matruh arrived in error at Sidi Barrani. These were hectic days indeed but come Christmas Day and each man had his Christmas fare as usual; even the piglet taken with them to fatten for the table had been considered as a possible substitute! But, no-one could bring themselves to kill it, so it became the Squadron mascot.

January 1936, both 'A' and 'HQ' Squadrons were now fully equipped and joined 'C' Squadron, whilst 'B' Squadron still awaiting their vehicles were to follow later. These troop movements left the Band and Rear Party to cope with the day to day running of the Barracks. Meanwhile, the bandsmen undertook driving instruction and First Aid Courses in training as stretcher bearers in the event of hostilities, for then the band would be disbanded. This baffled me rather, but I understood once it was explained to me that a Cavalry Band was not a War Office Establishment and was maintained by the Regiment as opposed to an Infantry Band.

We band Boys undertook the trumpet guards whilst the men catered with the other guard duties. Sporting activities for us continued. At this time great interest had been shown in the Small Bore Shooting Competition for Boys, which we were eventually to win, both the League and the Cup. In football we did well but were invariably beaten by the Infantry Teams who always fared better with their larger number of Boys from which to select a team.

On the Regiment's return to Barracks from the desert, further intensive training was carried out, this time the bandsmen were included. Three-day schemes were undertaken and they carried out duties as gunners, second drivers and, in some cases, driver. We, the Boys, carried on as usual. Amidst all these activities concern was mounting for the health of His Majesty King George V throughout the Empire and Commonwealth. On January 21st, 1936 we awoke to the sad news of his death. A big Memorial Parade was held in Abbassia Barracks. It was one of the biggest gatherings of troops ever seen in Cairo.

It was compulsory for Boys to attend education classes during the whole period of Boys' Service. Having come straight from school it wasn't difficult for me to get my Third Class Certificate and, after being taught the Regimental History, I quickly acquired my Second Class, but the First

Class was much more difficult. With all the schooling and tuition available I was certain I would eventually secure it.

Around the world there were rumblings of trouble. Spain had its Civil War, with the major powers all testing out their latest equipment in aid of one side or the other; Italy was fighting in Abyssinia and the Jews and Arabs were at each other's throats. It wasn't long before rumours were circulating about the Regiment leaving for Palestine. They turned out to be a little premature.

Once a year the Garrison Padre would take all the Boys of the Garrison on an annual trip to places of interest. This year it was to be the Pyramids and Sphinx. We all piled eagerly into the Regimental Bus, each with his haversack rations for the day, and set off. On arrival there we were escorted by a guide to explore the interior of the Pyramids. We entered and descended countless stairs, which went down and down, getting ever darker. The lit candles and paraffin lamps now giving only shadows as we proceeded downwards past the empty burial chambers. Some chambers housed empty coffins once occupied by one Pharaoh or other. I found it all very awesome, its size overwhelming. I now sought only to return to daylight and fresh air. As we emerged I joined the mad scramble to climb the largest Pyramid to see if we could reach the top. As opposed to going down and down inside, we now went up and ever upward (all fifty of us) but only a few made the top, the others conceding defeat. On reaching the summit we searched the weathered stone on which to carve our initials (like so many others before us) with our army issue jack knives. This done, we made the downward descent, a very formidable task indeed, and made for the comforts of the coach and the return journey back to Barracks.

It was early Spring when the natives of Egypt were thrown into mourning for the death of their King Fouad. This loss unleashed spontaneous demonstrations of mourning throughout the whole of Egypt, which made our presence in Cairo unwelcome; it would have been an intrusion into their national grief, so we were ordered to keep a low profile and remain in Barracks during the week of mourning. King Fouad's eldest son, fifteen-year-old Farouk, was being educated in England at Eton College and on May 6th he returned to Egypt to take on the responsibilities of State.

Our Officers were still playing Polo at Gazira and doing very well. When I was not on sport or duty I would spend a lot of time at the Stables watching the Farrier at work, which fascinated me, and during spells when the Regiment was out of Barracks, I would be allowed to exercise the Polo ponies which I enjoyed immensely. So I would be delighted whenever schemes or manoeuvres came around.

With winter sports out of the way we took to the summer sports of swimming and cricket, with me preparing for my Bronze Medal for Life-Saving and training for the Squadron Swimming Gala. By now I was well known throughout the Regiment, mainly through my sporting activities, so the rule about not communicating with the men of the Regiment went beside the board. The No Smoking rule was also broken, but not in public. Our Squadron (RHQ) held it's Swimming Gala and I came away with three prizes; for diving, backstroke and plate-lifting. This last event was a test of holding one's breath. Plates were thrown into the pool and one dived in and swam underwater to collect them. In the Regimental Swimming Gala I won the springboard and high diving events and came first in the Boy's Race. As you will agree, I was becoming very proficient at water sports. In the Inter-Band Swimming Contest, when the 7th and 8th Hussars and the 2nd Cheshire Regiment (the prime favourites) competed, we ran out the comfortable winners.

As Cairo was so hot and stuffy in Summer, the troops in the Garrison were allowed two weeks leave in Alexandria, a north coast town within easy reach of Cairo. This was known as 'the change of air'. The Band were luckier, because they would go to Alex for two weeks' duty, playing for the Married Personnel who had a Camp of their own. We also played for the Other Ranks on the beach in the morning and nightly in the Mess Tent. Having completed our fortnight's duties, we would then take our leave. The Camp had a long beach from which we would go fishing, surfing and swimming. It was a smashing break for the Boys as we were allowed into Alex provided we went with a bandsman. Sometimes we would go to the civilian beach which we preferred because of the 'female talent'. It was a very high class area known as 'Million Dollar Bay' (Stanley Bay). In the evening we would go into Alex to see the sights or to the all night swimming pool, where we were more likely to meet a nice girl, which of course I did – but it was a short-lived affair – purely a holiday romance. Throughout the summer, personnel would arrive for their 'change of air' at fortnightly intervals and on the last day but one before departure, the Commandment would hold a 'Tent Competition'. He inspected both inside and out. Many devices were thought up to win this competition such as, badges made out of bottle tops in the sand to enhance the approaches; tent ropes would be newly-washed; in fact literally no stone would be left unturned to outdo the other competitors. This year the Band ('A' Tent) won the competition. The prize was a fifty-akker NAAFI chit per person. This allowed the bearer fifty akkers' worth of goods in exchange for the chit, to be used in the NAAFI. Every soldier stationed in the Cairo was entitled to this break annually.

The rumours circulating about the Regiment going to Palestine were now to become fact.

Meanwhile, the newspapers from England were reporting a romance between His Majesty, King Edward VIII and an American Divorcee – a Mrs. Simpson – times were changing.

THE POLO TEAM HARD AT IT.

STABLE HANDS WITH THE POLO HORSES.

CHAPTER 7

Sporting events

At the end of June 1936, the Regiment received orders to go to Palestine to help suppress the disturbances between the Arabs and the Jews. Three days later 'B' Squadron were on their way as the 'Advance Party'. The remainder of the Regiment moved out three days after. This was the first operation as a complete mechanised unit. For this operation, the Band was as good as disbanded, temporarily, as they were dispatched to various Sabre Squadrons.

A 'Rear Party' was left behind to hold Main Barracks and to carry out what duties there were. Of course, we Boys were left behind and so, unfortunately, was the Bandmaster, just to ensure we didn't get into any mischief! One of the troopers who departed with the Regiment, owned a greyhound bitch, which he left in my care, so I had an excuse to 'go walk-about'. This I did quite often. With no official duties to carry out, the Bandmaster scratched his head to find us something to do. He eventually came up with the idea that we should paint the Bandroom, the Washroom and the Boys Room. This kept us busy for a few days.

In the middle of July, the 12th Lancers took over Main Barracks. I'm not sure why, but they didn't stay long. Whilst they were there I made a few friends who were in the Water Polo team. I would go as often as permitted to train with them and I learnt to play pretty well. Water polo is the dirtiest of all sports – what goes on under the water is nobody's business! I enjoyed this period and learned a lot about swimming. I had, by now, acquired my Silver Medal (Life-Saving). The Bandroom and Washroom were newly painted with just the Boys' Room to be done.

Every week our beds had to be debugged. This was a necessity in view of the prevalence of this common pest in Egypt. This entailed dismantling the iron bedstead, seeking out the bugs and their eggs and literally burning them with a blow-lamp. The mattress consisted of three 'biscuits'. These would be scrupulously cleaned with paraffin cloths with particular emphasis on all seams and corners. This was normally done on a Wednesday, however, whilst the Regiment were away the Quartermaster Staff decided to fumigate the whole Barracks: so we had another chore of closing all doors and windows of the entire Barracks and sealing them with tape. Before the final doors were sealed fumigating bombs were hurled in, releasing toxic gasses, which would take two whole days to take effect. Guess what? Yes, we had the job of unsealing and cleaning up.

Of an evening I would wander down to the Stables and perhaps get a ride on a Polo pony. This I did several times exercising Betsy, the greyhound, at the same time.

Men were coming back from Palestine in dribs and drabs and the rumour was that the Regiment was coming home soon. So I started boxing training with Jackie Sharman, our Inter-Services Featherweight Champion.

The Bandmaster was doing his crust because the Boys were not getting enough musical practice, so he arranged with the 7th Hussars that we practised with them. This we did and turned out for their Band Concerts. The summer passed all too quickly.

My debt was just about written off, so now I was able to make an allowance home to my Mother who, by the way, had been writing to me regularly keeping me in touch with events at home. My brother was now married with a little son and living at Shepperton, Middlesex, whilst my sister had settled to wedded bliss in Wokingham, Berkshire.

There were several civilian shops in the Garrison where one could buy almost anything, from a pair of shoes made-to-measure to an old banger of a car. The Bicycle Shop was the one most used by the Boys, because we could hire a bike by the hour for a few akkers. This was a very popular mode of transport in those days and we Boys found it gave us mobility. We could get all round the Garrison area and out into the desert to the RAF Camp at Heliopolis, a distance of about five miles.

Another popular shop was the Tattooist's. On one occasion, five of us Boys were going to The Slade Sports Ground to watch the Regimental Football team. As we passed the Tattooist we could see a guardsman being tattooed. We stood and watched for a while: suddenly he keeled over to the floor. I saw him going pale and as he keeled I laughed. One of my mates said, 'You shouldn't laugh, it's very painful.' He bet me I wouldn't have one put on. After offering to pay for the tattoo, I accepted his bet and nipped smartly into the shop: putting a brave face to my pals, I had a small one put on my upper left arm. Little did I know that that tattoo was going to get me into hot water in the near future.

Whilst the Regiment was in Palestine we had a new draft come to us from the 4th Hussars. So now I was not the youngest recruit. In fact, I felt quite an old soldier taking the new Boys around the Barracks.

The Regiment returned from Palestine in November with all sorts of stories of their exploits, after their first time on active service as a mechanised unit. They brought back a variety of souvenirs, such as Arab swords, daggers and Regimental badges made from Mother-of-Pearl and, of course, grapefruits and oranges. It was exactly one year after the Regiment's last Mounted Parade and they returned to find the 12th Lancers in occupation, but the two Regiments squeezed in together. Frantic efforts were made to erect tents on the sandy area opposite the Barracks; this would suffice for the two weeks, as the 12th Lancers would then be on the move again – this time to England.

Once settled in, the Regiment went full swing into a sports programme; Football, Boxing, Polo and Shooting. The Polo season started late because of the troubles in Palestine but once under way the teams soon got into their strides.

The subject of boxing cropped up again. The Regiment was forming a team for the Command Inter-Unit Championships. I was once again talked into having a go and so attended the team training sessions. Training was carried out instead of P.T. each morning and in the Garrison Gym in the evenings. Our first match was against the 11th Hussars and as I knew the Boys of the 11th, I felt that this time the odds were slightly more in my favour. I learnt that, as in my Regiment, the 11th only had one lad in Mosquito weight. He was about my size and weight so I was in with a chance, especially as I was a genuine Mosquito, had grown a bit and this time I had a singlet that fitted me, thanks to our heavyweight, Captain Harbord, who vividly remembered my earlier fiasco. He had a singlet made-to-measure for me.

On the night I turned up looking quite smart and looking the part. The team had done their best to see that I represented the Regiment in the best possible style. The fight started very calmly. I think he was a bit scared of me as I was of him, but we didn't dawdle too long. We both got stuck in and had a proper scrap. After three rounds, I was narrowly awarded the verdict. My seconds carried me shoulder high out of the ring. I had won my first fight! I felt very proud. This led to other bouts and I was entered for the Command Individuals.

My next fight came when the Regiment were drawn against the Manchester Regiment stationed at Moascar (in the Suez Canal Zone). The team travelled by train well aware of the reputation of the Manchesters, especially as their heavyweight was also the Heavyweight Champion of the Middle East. Formidable opposition indeed! Apparently, he was a giant of a man who went by the name of 'Tiny Williams'. Whilst I was waiting in their gym before the start of the contest, I felt quite confident, thanks to my intensive training, including my Badminton playing which had done much to make me quick and nimble on my feet. This essential asset would keep me out of trouble, I hoped.

'Who am I fighting?' I asked my seconds.

'Don't worry, Tich, you've got an easy fight. You've been drawn against Tiny Williams,' they said.

I relaxed. A few minutes later the gym door opened and in walked 'Goliath'.

'That's him,' said my second.

'That's Tiny Williams?' I asked. I couldn't believe my eyes. I stood glued to the floor. How did he pass as a Mosquito, I asked myself. Maybe their scales were different to ours. Such were the thoughts going through my head when I was summoned to the ring. Was I relieved when I saw my opponent get into the other corner – a lad, the same shape and size as myself.

Each boxer wore a coloured sash peculiar to his coloured corner and on the corner posts would be a light bulb of his own colour, which was lit at the end of the fight indicating the winner. The fight, although for only three rounds, was a rough one. I got hurt, but I hurt him as well, even more so. At the final bell we awaited the decision and both my seconds and I thought I had won.

'Red is the winner,' called the judge.

'That's me!' I'd won! Imagine my disappointment when the blue light came on declaring my opponent the winner – I had lost.

November 1936 and I was now seventeen years old, five feet one inch tall and slightly heavier. I had achieved much in sport and was doing well in music, so much so that I was under consideration to be entered as a pupil at The Royal Military School of Music – Kneller Hall. I had also acquired two subjects of my Fist Class Certificate of Education and was still continuing my schooling. All in all, things were going well with just about a year to go before I came on Man's Service.

The Band's routine was continuing as usual. One particular Saturday we were playing at the Heliopolis Race Course, and during a break in the musical programme, someone asked if anybody had seen the tattoo Boy Napier had on his arm. That started things going! The Bandmaster, who was seated near me, turned and asked 'Is it true about you having a tattoo?' How could I hide anything like that, so I replied 'Yes, Sir.' 'Report to my office tomorrow.'

Came the dawn, the Bandmaster's Office and trouble. He inspected the offending tattoo then called me all the stupid, idiotic and ridiculous things he could lay his tongue to and, finally, awarded me six months extra fatigues. In the main, jobs done on fatigues were usually dirty and strenuous chores of which a Cavalry Regiment had plenty, but with no horses these were somewhat limited: so I was put to cleaning the tubular bells. I decided to do this chore in the Washroom, which incidentally was adjacent to the Bandroom, and so I thought would be convenient. After dinner, with all the bandsmen enjoying an afternoon's snooze, I set to work, overlooking the fact that the Washroom being empty made any sounds echo! So, as the bells pealed out I was confronted with repeated interruptions; first by one angry bandsman and then another, so I beat a hasty retreat and returned the tubular bells to the Stores.

The following day I was detailed to clean the windows in the Mens' Barrack Room. This was again after the mid-day meal with the men partaking of their afternoon snooze. I crept in with my gear, amid snores and grunts, and proceeded with everything going well; my aim being not to awaken anyone. But alas! that was not to last. I slipped. My boot went through the window-pane making one hell of a noise. There were shouts of protest calling me some very unflattering names, then all was quiet again. Crash! I had dropped my bucket of water. That was too much. I fled to the quiet of the Boys' Room. There were two or three other similar incidences and with so many complaints reaching the Bandmaster that their afternoon rest period was being frequently disturbed, to please everybody the Bandmaster reduced my six-month fatigue period to three further days.

When we returned from the Races late one Saturday afternoon the situation in the Barracks was chaotic. Apparently, the NAAFI Warehouse and Headquarters had had a fire, which incidentally was a few hundred yards from the Main Barracks. It appears that everyone in the Regiment, who was not otherwise engaged, rushed to give a hand and help where they could. It soon transpired that the only help that was given was to help empty the Warehouse. Men were seen riding Ice Cream Tricycles full of loot, pedalling like hell back to Barracks; others were seen carrying mattress cases full of whatever they could carry and then back again for more. The tricycles would make a quick turn around after depositing their loot; men were working in pairs, one upstairs throwing out the goods whilst the other would load up and make off in haste once fully loaded. It was some while before the Military Police realised what was going on before calling a halt to it. The fire had completely gutted the buildings in the 'Imperial Court Area' and for a long time it was apparent that any cigarettes smoked were of the 'Imperial' variety, whilst a lot of personnel not hitherto seen in civvies would be seen in what was nicknamed the 'Imperial' suit. Investigations followed which recovered a considerable amount of the stolen goods and charges were made, but needless to say for every case the Police brought there were no witnesses.

Before we ease into the summer sports there was one more boxing event to take place. This was the Command Individuals for which I had been entered. These championships cover a period of weeks and in April they come to a head with all the prospective champions fully trained and keyed up, of which I was one. At the weigh-in, I learned that there was only myself and one other Boy qualified for the Mosquito title, so our contest would be in the final. We had a full week of boxing with the finals taking place on Friday and Saturday. The Band was to play on the Final Night so I would be excused, I thought. I fought my contest the previous night and won, which made me the Mosquito Champion of the Middle East. It had been a hard fight leaving me in a bit of a mess. My lips were badly cut making it impossible for me to play my instrument; nevertheless, I was feeling pretty pleased with myself. On the Saturday the Band rehearsed for the evening programme. I thought I would be able to relax and watch the remaining bouts, but no, the Bandmaster had other ideas. He sent me to the drummer to help out where I could on the cymbals, triangle and other sound effects required. The boxing season ended with the Regiment finishing third in the Regimental League and taking three individual titles, mine being one of them.

I soon learned that when one joins an Irish Regiment, March 17th was an annual event not to be missed for that is St. Patrick's Day. It turned out to be a strenuous day for the Band. It started with an early Reveille with a mug of tea laced with rum and of course those Bandsmen who could had more than tea. That over, our first call would be to the Officers' Mess to awaken them with a medley of Irish tunes, stopping at each individual bedroom. Then we would give a concert to the Other Ranks while they took their breakfast. Our next function was at 10 a.m. when we were expected to perform at the Regimental Football Match – Officers versus Other Ranks. This match always started off as a football match, that is the whistle was blown to commence battle, and that was the only legal event. The rest of the game was an 'All-In' affair, with everyone dressed just as they pleased and all football rules going beside the board. There were no restrictions on the number of players on each side, anyone who wanted to play just got stuck in. There were always ambulances standing by and usually if the drivers got bored they too would join in the affray. Meanwhile, the Band played on as the spectacle moved first from one end of the pitch then to the other. At no time did we see the ball – perhaps they were playing without one! This fracas continued for almost two hours but we played on as each side wheeled and reeled to and fro. I remember thinking it was going to take a salvo from the Royal Horse Artillery to stop this madness when miraculously and very suddenly the field cleared and lo and behold there stood the Commanding Officer tied to one goal-post and the Adjutant to the other. Similarly the other goal-posts were bedecked with the Medical Officer and the Padre. I almost forgot to mention the few casualties stretched out on the field. They were all hustled into the ambulances none the worse for the experience we were to hear later. As we marched off I was told there would be a rescue mission to free the Officers who would, in fact, next appear officially at lunch. I think they were pulling my leg! On returning to Barracks we saw evidence that someone else had come in for a bit of stick – the Provost Sergeant's trousers had replaced the Regimental Flag! At the end of the day there had been no actual murders committed, or at least none were recorded. Needless to say, with the annual football match out of the way the bars were open to everyone (except Boys). The next highlight of the day would be the Open Air Band Concert on the Square in the evening. With this behind us we could then consider ourselves officially off duty. This was the usual procedure with a few variations for a Paddy's Day which each year was looked forward to eagerly, when discipline and routine were allowed to lapse.

April 1937 and another draft arrived; this time from the 3rd Hussars. Among the Boys that came were two good footballers who arrived in time to help us win the Boys' League for the first time. Also, during the same season the Band were runners-up in the Inter-Troop Cup; Boy Prescott won the Regimental Discus, Hammer and Shot. He was six feet two inches yet he was not the tallest Boy we had – and I was no longer the shortest.

Still not being old enough to officially smoke it wasn't very strange that the Band Corporal would periodically search my person and my locker. So it came about that I practically kept him in cigarettes. He would confiscate them, give me a clip around the ear and then all would be well until the next time. The punishment meted out to Boys for very frivolous things was, to say the least, ridiculous; for example, on a Sunday when our Band was on duty, a section performed in the

Church and the remainder of the Band personnel would act as the choir. Occasionally I might be seen to yawn and be almost lulled to sleep. If I was seen I would have to report to the Band Office after the service and the Band Corporal would then give me a good hiding. Eventually, this happened just once too often. While he was laying into me I felt I'd had enough of this, so when he was totally unprepared I lunged at him with a straight left and a right hook, which caught him right in the mouth. He stood back aghast and then frantically looked around for something to strike me with, but before he could find anything I opened the door and bolted. That was the last time he ever thumped me.

From the various paying concerts we were giving I was now able to save enough money to buy my own clarinet. I was given permission by the Bandmaster to go into Cairo with a colleague to look over the clarinets displayed in the two main musical shops. I eventually settled for a new model which had all the keys padded instead of holes. This was very satisfying, especially as I was now playing on the Solo Clarinet stand.

Two of our Solo clarinet players had recently returned to England on demob. Other losses we suffered through these periodic departures affected our sporting events too. My dear friend and boxing partner, Jackie Sharman, left for Blighty and so did our Regimental Football Captain, Jimmy Paviour. He left and eventually joined an Amateur Football Club in England and he was subsequently to captain the England Amateur side. It was sad and unsettling to see these familiar faces departing for the UK which brings to mind the following verses I had read in our Regimental Journal; it was called 'Time Expired' and went like this:

'I've packed my kit, it's labelled up, I've handed in my spurs,
I've said goodbye to the 'Wet Canteen' for better or for worse,
My credits have been squared up and I've withdrawn all my pay,
For I'm 'Time-expired', I'm going home and I sail for Blighty today.

I've just forgotten how many times I've said 'Roll on the boat'
And now its here, it seems so queer, that it gets me in the throat,
And though the Blighty I've dreamt of don't seem far away,
I almost wonder whether I am glad that I'm going home today.

My halfback is standing over there waiting to say goodbye,
His time ain't up till next year, and that's what makes him sigh,
I remember when he first came up, for we 'mucked in' right away,
And for five long years we've been as one, now its got to end today.

We did our training, we were taught our drills, he was better than I by far,
And after he had been at 'duty' for about twelve months, they offered
        him the 'Bar',
But he knew I'd never get a stripe, so he threw his chance away,
And we soldiered on as 'Troopers', right until today.

We've lain side by side 'neath tropical skies, when its been too hot to 'kip',
And the howling of the Piards has given us the pip,
We used to talk of the folks at home, and of the happy times we spent,
It was here whilst in the Army that I learnt what 'Friendship' meant.

And now the time is drawing near, they are falling in the band,
And my heart it feels as heavy as lead, as I shake my Buddy's hand,
But the time will pass and when he's through, he'll see me again, so he
        says,
And we'll forget that we are back in 'Civvy Street' when we talk of those
        khaki days.'

Sometimes we would get excellent replacements in the drafts and so it was with some losses and some gains that the Regiment carried forward it's sporting programmes.

The cricket season was with us again and it was not one of my pet sports. As I have said before, I was always prepared to have a go. Had the Boys' team been selected, I don't think I would have been included but being as we could only produce a full team with me, there was little choice. Being devoid of instruction or coaching I had not even acquired the art of wielding the bat. I felt lumbered with a full size bat plus the pads that came up to my thighs and bore no resemblance to the contours of my short legs. I didn't bowl but was pretty agile in the field. My batting left something to be desired and warranted only tenth or eleventh in the batting order. Nevertheless, whatever was bowled at me my bat would automatically become horizontal to the ground as I'd take a swipe – no matter where the ball was pitched.

Once, I actually scored the winning runs. It was against the 7th Hussars on a hard sand pitch covered with coconut matting. I went in as eleventh man with a total of twelve runs needed to win. The opposition must have rubbed their hands with glee when they saw me coming out for they knew I did not excel as a cricketer from previous games played with them. To dispose of us 'tail-enders' they put on their best bowlers – Mick Morris and Pedlar Palmer, (both of these Boys played for their Regiment later). Mick tossed one up. I didn't give it a chance to bounce. I took two paces down the wicket and made an almighty swing at it; it connected and went on for four – first blood. The second ball was somewhat faster. I took my usual swing but it whizzed straight through to the wicket keeper. Likewise, the third ball. The fourth scored a further four whilst the fifth I was able to run for two, having survived a dropped catch. Only two more wanted to win, with excitement mounting. The last ball was high and slow to fool me but down the wicket I went, connected and gave it an mighty slam. The bowler Mick watched it race through to the boundary. We had won and I had scored my highest score to date.

THE BAND FOOTBALL TEAM INTER-TROOP RUNNERS-UP 1937.

THE REGIMENTAL SWIMMING TEAM THE 'BOY' FRONT RIGHT.

CHAPTER 8

Things go swimmingly

After nearly three years in Egypt I was feeling somewhat like an old soldier. I had my 2 Year Service Stripe, commonly called a 'Dodger' and was travelling around Egypt on various sporting events seeing quite a lot of the Egyptian life-style. I was also getting quite conversant with the Arabic language; unfortunately, the swear words came first and I could now swear in Arabic for five minutes non-stop, without repeating myself. The natives used swear words as everyday language. I later broadened my lingual prowess on a par equal to that of the natives. This was mainly through necessity when bargaining with the traders. At least now I could hold my own, secure a good deal and make myself understood into the bargain.

There was more trouble at this time in Cairo; the students were rioting again. This time there appeared to be good reason. The Boy King Farouk was flexing his muscles. He just up and sacked his Prime Minister, Nahas Pasha, much to the surprise of the British Ambassador. This caused much bad feeling with the British Government and throughout Egypt. He had been a popular Prime Minister with the large majority of the natives, and his Party held a majority in the Egyptian Parliament.

In England, Edward VIII had abdicated and May 1937 saw the Coronation of King George VI. In Egypt, the British troops held parades and tattoos to mark the occasion. Such displays were always well attended by the civilian populations. It provided them with a spot of colour and excitement in their rather drab lives. We went to Alexandria to take part in a Tattoo to be held there at the Race Course. It was a searchlight affair and the theme was the British Army of the past; a truly spectacular sight. It was during these performances that our solo cornet player used the silver 'Herald Trumpet' which had not been used since the Regiment were in India. This trumpet was presented to the Regiment at the Delhi Durbar in 1911 and was kindly loaned for the occasion by the Commanding Officer. We performed three nights with rehearsals each morning, with the afternoons as leisure. We could either go into town or to the beach. It was chilly for swimming so I decided to try my hand at fishing. On the beach was an old man who had a small shed cluttered with all varieties of fishing tackle (including live bait) that we could hire. I spent hours enjoying my new-found sport. Whilst in Alexandria we were challenged to a Water Polo Match against HMS *Gloworm*, a British Destroyer anchored in the harbour. We lost but the invitation to go aboard after the match was much appreciated. All good things come to an end and we had to return to Barracks and back to mundane routine. For me, life was good. The hot weather suited me down to the ground and the routine of band duties followed by sport was idyllic. I can honestly say that I loved the life style.

This year, my love of swimming was amply rewarded when I was selected to represent the Regiment in the Swimming Team as their first string, Spring Board and three meter High Board Diving, also as first leg in any Boys' Race. I was considered too small for competition Water Polo so my games in that were very limited. The team used to travel all over Egypt for Regimental Galas and for Egyptian Championships as well. It was during one of these galas that I was watched by the 1936 Olympic Diving Champion, Pete De Jardine, who was touring the Middle East giving exhibitions; I was introduced to him by our Swimming Officer. He had been very impressed with my performance.

'Who is coaching you?' was one of the questions he asked me.

'Nobody,' I said.

He then turned to our Officer and suggested that I should be taken in hand and be taught the finer arts of diving in order that I might be brought up to Olympic standard for 1940. A coach was found. He was a Sergeant Major in the Royal Signals who was at one time the British Champion. There were too many obstacles for us to get together very often, although I had obtained special permission from my CO – my band duties, and his duties and the availability of the swimming pool never seemed to coincide, so I didn't get my tuition. I was very frustrated and in sheer desperation I turned to the Egyptian Champion, then serving with the Egyptian Army in Heliopolis. I had met him previously in several competitions and when he heard of my predicament was only too pleased to help. His coaching certainly paid dividends for when I entered the All-Egyptian Championships held later in the year, I came second to him with only one point in it. I was greatly encouraged.

Another feature that crept in was Tombola. Every Tuesday evening the Regiment held a session on the Square, with a bar available. The troops responded with a very high attendance; this new form of entertainment soon caught on. On Wednesdays, the Royal Tank Regiment held their session on the Square, which was next to ours. Thursday was 'Concert Night' and Fridays everyone would descend on the 7th Hussars for their Tombola Session. In fact, entertainment was arranged for every night of the week to give the troops an alternative to the pleasures of Cairo, as V.D. was so rife. It was on one of these concerts that I had an embarrassing accident. The Band dress for these concerts was 'Blues'; Blue Jacket, Overalls and Spurs. My position when playing was in the front row about the middle, right in front of the Bandmaster. From that position I was allotted the task of changing the Bandmaster's music sheet after each number.

On this particular occasion, as usual, I stood up, placed my clarinet on my chair, took a pace forward and changed the music. Having completed this chore I took a pace backwards, or rather that was my intention, but my spurs had become crossed and instead of taking a step backwards, I fell heavily onto my chair. There was an almighty CRACK! My clarinet was broken in two. I stood up and picked up the two halves. There was a hushed silence; my face reddened to scarlet and the audience stared aghast. The Bandmaster scowled and said 'Get back to the drummer and give him a hand.' The concert continued. That performance, I added the 'bird whistle' to my repertoire of sound effects! But not quite so simple was paying for the damage done to my instrument. Not all Band functions were as catastrophic as that.

I remember, with nostalgia, the twice yearly events of the troops' 'Day Out' to The Aswan Dam Barrage. This was a huge structure built across the Nile, with it's surrounding area laid out into magnificent gardens. During the leisurely cruise, some four hours long, on a luxurious pleasure boat complete with a licensed bar, the Band was engaged to play, but once we arrived at The Barrage we, along with everyone else, would disembark and go our separate ways. There were donkey carriages for hire and several other amusements, also a tour round the beautiful gardens. Of course, there were always those who drank too much, who would hire a boat and take on the currents of the Nile! They invariably finished up at the Medical Centre, receiving a course of injections against nearly every known infectious disease after having fallen in the river. The blue Nile was anything but blue at that point! The donkey races were a great favourite with the ex-cavalry personnel too, with many showing off their prowess. After a day of good clean fun we would embark for the trip up river and again we would perform for the troops whilst they drank and supped up the beauty of a floodlit river Nile; a most pleasurable day indeed. We would also go through the same routine for the married families on their trip to the barrage once a year.

1937 was my last year on Boys' Service but I had to wait until my eighteenth birthday in November before that was to become reality. In the meantime, I was to carry on with my education completing my studies for my First Class Certificate; increasing my knowledge of music and improving my performance on the clarinet, with intense training to be continued in my swimming in readiness for the 1940 Olympics. So, this year was to be a very busy and arduous one – but what a prize at the end – Mans' Service.

Earlier in the year I spent four weeks in The Citadel Military Hospital. Whilst we were moving the piano down to the Square for the usual concert, my foot got caught under it. Three toes were wrenched back and broken. I was to have my very first ever period in hospital. I was given a blue uniform and a list of orders. The discipline was very strict; so much so that one hardly dared to move from one's bed for fear of breaking some rule or other. I struck up a pretty good relationship with one of the Nursing Sisters. Had I been on Mans' Service something might have come of it, but this was not to be. Instead I took to watching the Bridge School every evening and by the time I was discharged I could play to a reasonable standard.

On my return to Barracks I got down seriously to my swimming and diving training. The Officers were still winning all sorts of trophies on the Polo Field. At the International Match played at Gazira Sporting Club we were asked to give a display of marching as a massed Band together with the 7th and 11th Hussars and the Drums of the Northumberland Fusiliers. This proved rather a novelty as such a sight had not been seen before, and judging by the fan mail received by the Bandmaster, we were to be in great demand in the future. A selection of music was played during the afternoon, which was much appreciated by the spectators.

One line of sport which I had no inclination to take part in was track and field events, although I had to enter into the Boys' Race. This race was won by my schoolmate Spike, who was proving himself a pretty good sprinter. Another Boy, John Prescott, was still doing his stuff with the Discus and Hammer, winning all the Regimental events with distances of 92 ft. and 89 ft. respectively.

My finances were improving. Apart from my normal wages, still at one shilling a day, there were the paid Band engagements. I was also earning a bit on the side by doing trumpet guards for the men at one pound a time; I would sometimes fit in two guards a week. In addition, I also helped at the Tombola Sessions, selling tickets etc, which would make me a further £1 per session. Altogether, this made me a fairly rich Band Boy. With this newly-found wealth I bought myself a bicycle, which I hired out on occasions. This gave me greater mobility with my very tight work schedule and was of great benefit to me in my leisure time. When time permitted, I would sit in at the card school and watch the Bandsmen play their favourite card game of Nap, so that when I was on Mans' Service I would be able to join the card school.

Life was going along swimmingly, when instructions were received that the Band personnel was to have a month's intensive military training, so the Band routine as we knew it was disrupted. The schedule was to include: driving; maintenance; foot drill; flag-bashing (messages sent by means of flags); bayonet drill; stretcher drill; instructions on the Vickers Berthier light machine gun; map reading; sand-table work; message writing; grenade training and anything else they could fit in! Although it was rough on the Bandsmen, they appeared to enjoy themselves. Of course, it made a change from the monotony of Band practice and although nobody knew it at the time, it was to stand them in good stead in the very near future. While they were undergoing their training we, the Boys, were having intensive training into the theory of music. Being as I was now on the Solo Clarinet stand, I was set some very difficult exercises by the Bandmaster in readiness for our return to the United Kingdom. The normal routine of a Cavalry Regiment was a three year tour in Egypt, followed by an even longer period in India. As we were now mechanised, this ruled out the tour to India so the far-sighted persons were now preparing for a return home.

At this time I was getting the impression that the Bandmaster was beginning to change his mind about me. He had, in the past, considered me a little so-and-so, always up to some mischief or other and often getting into trouble; (I'm sure I don't know why!) but now he was giving me private clarinet lessons and he even offered me a new clarinet. This instrument was the new Bohem system. I declined; I preferred my own which surprised him. I was no fool; having my own instrument I could avoid the various inspections on band instruments and in the event of accident or damage also avoid unnecessary trouble.

If and when the Band returned to England, the duties of the Band would be vastly different from those in Egypt. There would be long engagement seasons throughout the summer when we would be away from the Regiment for four or five months at a time, touring the seaside towns playing programmes on the Bandstands, which was a popular feature of nearly all seaside resorts. In addition, there would be other concerts and functions held in the evenings, which sometimes would entail staying two or three weeks in a town and then moving on to another. This could be a very lucrative time for the Bandsmen and the Band Fund. I had never experienced an 'Engagement Season' in England so I was looking forward to returning home and, of course, it would be great to see the family again. This I learned later was all wishful thinking.

THE BAND BOYS - 1937.

CHAPTER 9

Almost a man

Life in Egypt was carrying on as normal. I now had my Silver Medal in Lifesaving. Our football team was somewhat depleted with several Boys having reached Mans' Service. Very few of their replacements were sport-minded but we struggled through although we didn't achieve much success; only in swimming did we have any success. I was picked for the Band team in the Inter-Troop football where we reached the final, but were beaten 2-1. As I would be on Man's Service when the finals of the boxing came, I would be allowed to defend my Mosquito weight title, so of course I carried on training.

Since mechanisation it was found necessary for the Regiment to learn new foot drill, so whilst the Bandsmen were undergoing their intensive training we had to do a spell on the Square learning new drills. Also, the wearing of riding breeches was no longer permitted.

After all the military training was over, the band settled down to the normal routine again. We had a 'First' in that we had a date to broadcast over the E.S.B. (Egyptian State Broadcasting). We were also practising like mad because we were going to make a record of the descriptive piece of music

The Three Bears. We played that piece over and over; so many times in fact that I was hearing it in my sleep. On the day of the recording we went to a Studio in Cairo and after a certain amount of aggravation, we settled down to do the recording but, oh dear, what a bother! On six occasions the playback had picked up extraneous noises and so we would have to start all over again. Finally, the desired recording was achieved and we were all very relieved. The number two side took a little less time and we finished up with a record we were all very proud of.

One small annoyance which used to gall us Boys was that we, 15, 16 and 17 year olds had to be in bed at 9.30 p.m. every night whilst the Married Families' children aged between 8 and 14 years were playing outside our windows till all hours.

Throughout the football season it was usual for someone to be running a Sweepstake in the Regiment. There was a Sweep for the highest score and also the Pontoon Sweep where one picked a team and the first team to score twenty-one goals won but it had to be twenty-one dead; if you went over the twenty-one you carried on to forty-two, which very rarely happened. I would always have a go (on the quiet) and on one weekly Sweep when I drew Raith Rovers, they scored seven goals; this netted me about £E10. Then, on another occasion I won the Pontoon Sweep which netted me about £E25. Of course, it became general knowledge and the Bandmaster when he heard of it actually congratulated me on my win. He only needed one to win himself, so I reckon the congratulations were possibly begrudgingly given! However, I pocketed the winnings. Often when a man in the Regiment was broke or had something of comparative value he would raffle it (you know the type!): well, from one such raffle I won a Spanish guitar. I tried hard to play, but didn't get much encouragement; neither did I have an instruction book whereby I could teach myself; so I eventually got rid of it. Of course, in every Regiment you would get the 'wide boy'. We had one who would, nearly every week raffle a £E1 at five piastas a go. He reckoned he made at least £5 every time.

The summer of 1937 was a hectic one for the Band. Apart from their normal musical duties they were going on three-day schemes with the duty troops; there was also the annual rifle range details where every man had to fire a course and obtain a certain percentage to qualify for extra pay.

The sports programme was being carried on whenever possible in view of the intensive training. I was still doing well in the swimming pool and in fact this year I won every diving competition I entered at the Command Individuals swimming event, as well as diving, in the Boys' race I came second to Boy Goulding (Irish Guards). This lad went on to break every short distance record in the Army Record Book. I kept running up against these Irish Guards Boys, who had the beating of me. Remember my first fight in the ring?

Our 'change of air' leave at Alex came early this year with an extra week. Cairo was having its usual sandstorms when we left and the heat was most oppressive; so the beaches of Alex made a welcome change where the air was cooler and we could enjoy the pleasures of surfing and fishing, along with midnight bathing. Again, our little old man on the beach hired us the surfboards and fishing gear. We formed quite a friendship with this little man and used to look forward to seeing him from time to time. He could spin us a few yarns about his fishing days and gave us a few fishing tips into the bargain. It was whilst fishing that I caught more than I had bargained for on one occasion. I proceeded to cast, took a big backward swing, then threw the weight into the sea, or at least that was my intention. I felt that I'd caught something to my rear. I turned to see one of my mates well and truly hooked by his top lip, flailing at the air. I hastened to his aid, recovered my hook, but my mate was very sore about the whole thing. Nevertheless, we went on to enjoy the rest of our holiday period. We had the usual Tent Competition whilst we were there and again the Band came out tops.

Time was passing and it wouldn't be long before I was on Man's Service; that being the case I started taking a few chances, for example, one Saturday morning when all the inspections were over, I went to the NAAFI (still out of bounds to me) chatted to the troops and got myself invited to play a game of billiards. I was engrossed in the game and enjoying a cigarette at the same time, when an awkward shot presented itself. After much thought I decided the only way I could reach that shot was to sprawl over the table. Poised set to strike and saying 'I'll get this bloody shot if it kills me,' I was gripped by the feet and yanked off the table by NCO in charge Boys, standing there with a big grin on his face.

'You're not on Man's Service yet,' he said 'Get up to your room.'

Off I went. I was in big trouble. I could get done for (1) being in the NAAFI, (2) associating with the men, (3) playing billiards, (4) smoking, (5) swearing; that was just about the lot which must get me a round of fatigues. At the same time I could think of a few reasons why I might get away with it, if I played my cards right. First of all, I had a boxing title to defend in the current boxing competitions ahead and the Commanding Officer had given special dispensation to the title holders to go on training sessions; therefore, if I was put on fatigues during my off-duty period I could still go to the training sessions. In fact, I was fined £3 so I didn't have to worry about the fatigues after all.

About this time a new order appeared on the Regimental Orders Board. It originated from the Government in London and was in effect that all Boys serving in H.M. Forces should have a free pint of milk daily. As a result of this momentous decision, each day including Sundays, at 10.30 a.m. all Boys throughout the Army were paraded to the Cookhouse for their milk ration. I wondered if at last somebody in high office had realised that we Boys were undernourished, underfed, underpaid and overworked!

The Individual Boxing Championships were now in full swing. I had a bye in the first round and won my next fight, which put me in the semi-finals; won that and once again I was in the final which was to take place on November twenty-fifth. Meanwhile, I had become a MAN – a transition which cannot be imagined by anyone, except those who have passed through it. It compares with taking a leap from Hell into Heaven!

Before I finally made it, I recall one incident which shows the petty meanness of certain individuals. My eighteenth birthday was on November 2nd, 1937. I went to bed on the night before, as usual with my kit cleaned and ready for inspection, knowing that from midnight I was on MANS'

SERVICE; I bought myself a packet of cigarettes and a lighter and these I put in my locker unopened ready for the morning, when it would be 'legal' for me to 'light up'. In came the NCO at 9.30 sharp and proceeded to inspect our kit. After checking that my kit was satisfactory, he opened my locker, saw the cigarettes and took them out. He turned to me and said 'Are you on Mans' Service yet?'

'Tomorrow,' I replied.

'You're not entitled to have these until tomorrow,' he said and then walked off with them. On the morrow I'd be a MAN.

I had my kit packed ready to move from the Boys' Quarters as soon as possible, which I did with all speed before taking breakfast. I went to the NCO who had done the previous night's inspection.

'Can I have my fags and lighter?' I asked.

To my surprise he just handed them over to me. I lit one up in front of him and left to collect my civvy suit, which I had stashed away some weeks earlier with one of the Bandsmen, who incidentally had sold it to me. I was then allotted a bed in the Mens' Barrack Room and with several of the ex-Boys arranged a night out in Cairo. We all went down to the NAAFI where I could legally now go, at the start of the night's proceedings. The Manager bought me my first beer, he being a keen boxing fan of mine; he had in fact followed my progress for the past three years. The beer I drank under sufferance; I didn't like it at all.

Once on Mans' Service all sorts of things changed. My pay trebled, I was allowed out of Barracks during my leisure time without a chaperone and in civvies. I was already detailed for a three-day scheme attached to 'C' Squadron as a Trumpeter, but that wasn't for two weeks. I realised almost immediately that being a 'Trooper' wasn't going to lighten my work load, nevertheless there were many freedoms which more than compensated that meant more scope to enjoy life.

My first night on the town wasn't too exciting mainly because I didn't drink but we, that is three ex-Boys and myself, did a tour of the town with me togged up in my civvies. We went to a Cabaret at The Globe Theatre where we watched, mesmerised, the traditional 'belly-dancing' being performed. It was fantastic. Then on to the bars and cafes where we met men of the Regiment all eager to buy me drinks and some even offered to take me to the brothel area. Of course, I'd heard of the infamous Sharia Wagh-El-Birka (the street where every house was a brothel registered with the authorities), but I was not too keen to lose my virginity in such circumstances, but no doubt that would go there in time. I was, of course, scared to death; the thought of catching VD,after all the lectures I had had in the past, was a prime factor in my reluctance to indulge. I enjoyed myself immensely nevertheless, and my newly-found freedoms. Going into Cairo in civvies and not returning to Barracks until midnight.... this indeed was LIVING!

EGYPTIAN VERSION OF A FAMOUS BRITISH STORE...

CHAPTER 10

All kinds of training

A variety of new interests opened up to me now that I was released from the restrictions of Boy's Service and it wasn't long before I was inveigled into the Nap School where I paid to learn the game. Fortunately, I learn very quickly when I'm interested in a thing so it didn't cost me too dear. I spent many hours from then on playing cards and eventually progressed on to Bridge. There was always some card game or other going on where one could lose their money if so inclined.

I successfully defended my Mosquito title and became Champion of the Middle East for the second time. I was immediately approached by the Squadron (RHQ) to box in the Inter-Squadron boxing match, This I agreed to do with some reluctance because I didn't fancy my chances in the Mens' weights being so undersized. I fathomed out that I would always be on the wrong end of a long straight left, nevertheless, I agreed.

Coming on to Mans' Service might have released me from trivial rules and regulations but also it gave me added duties, as I very soon found out. The intensive military training that the Bandsmen had recently undergone I was now to learn and as quickly as possible get up to their standard. The Square bashing was the hardest, especially when they gave me a rifle. This I found very heavy and after the first few rifle drills I was exhausted. I also had to fire a course on the rifle in order to qualify for an extra 3d. per day. Life certainly wasn't any easier, but at least there was plenty of variety.

Next came the driving instructions. These were carried out in a Morris 15 cwt. – not the easiest of vehicles to learn on but I soon got the hang of it. There was a particular problem I had to contend with, my legs were somewhat too short; but the fitters came up with a solution. They made me a couple of blocks that I could put on the pedals: that made driving much easier.

Christmas was once again with us and the usual goings on were well advanced. The Dining Rooms were always decorated with paper garlands giving a most festive appearance; this was undertaken every year by volunteers from the band. In addition, the troops were encouraged to make their contribution to the over-all seasonal decorations of the Dining Room. These would appear in the form of a blanket pinned to the wall and decorated with cotton wool depicting some scene or event which had occurred within the Regiment during the past year, with seasonal greetings to the 8th Hussars. The dinner was the usual Christmas repast and on this occasion it would be served up by the Officers and members of the Sergeants Mess.

After Christmas we got down to some serious training in the Western desert. The Band personnel was distributed among the Sabre Squadrons and the schemes lasted weeks instead of days. I went out with 'C' Squadron as a trumpeter and as a second gunner on the V.B. gun. The ride in the back of a pick-up across miles and miles of desert was no joke. One soon learns that the desert is not all sand, but miles of rocks and camel shrub which makes for a most uncomfortable and unpleasant ride. You could get over a lot of the discomfort if you packed the kit and equipment in a certain way with the bedding on top so as to make a comfortable position in which to relax. It had been known for men to actually sleep on such a journey and such was the case with my fellow traveller whilst on a trip to Mersa Matruh.

Both of us were relaxing in the back as much as one could relax on a very rough journey: he had dozed off as we struck the salt flats. These are so smooth that from the lying down one could think we had come to a halt. My mate thought just that. Whilst we were travelling at about forty-five miles per hour and without previous warning, he just leapt over the side – a latrine stop – he thought. As he hit the ground he was hurled over and over, his legs unable to meet the momentum.

'Man overboard!' I yelled.

The driver backed to where my mate lay. He was in one hell of a mess and all he kept saying was 'I thought we'd stopped.'

Fortunately, he suffered no serious injury other than a thorough grazing which had been the reason for the heavy bleeding. I felt sure that had he been able to keep upright and on his feet he would have broken every track record in the book!

The nights on the desert were pretty cold, especially at this time of year, so we usually went to bed fully dressed, wrapped in the few blankets allowed. The scorpions, centipedes, lizards and the snakes would often take advantage of the warmth and get in alongside. This could be hair-raising experience but with a cool head and nerve one could survive the perils of the desert. As only two of the crew of four could bed down in the back of the car, it befell the two juniors to face this added danger.

On this particular exercise, the Regiment was carrying out several functions apart from the schemes and manoeuvres with other Regiments. They were also to carry out reconnaissance marches on various parts of the desert of which little or nothing was known. This was to be of immense value in the years to come. At the same time they were also able to learn about the hazards and tricks of the Western desert, which was to stand them in good stead in the very near future. Our food rations were of a basic nature and were usually augmented by the crew pooling their cash and purchasing extras in Cairo prior to leaving for the desert. Our cooking facilities were a bit primitive but like all cavalry men one soon learnt to improvise. I soon learnt to cook. With a primus stove and a fire made from, a half petrol can filled with sand, then soaked with petrol (the Benghazi Cooker), one could usually turn out a good cup of tea and an edible meal. After many meals like this I was becoming a dab hand with the 'skillet'. After a week in the desert, which had been quite an experience, we returned to Cairo to resume where we had left off.

On our return, I was told by the Bandmaster that a Nursing Sister had been enquiring after me. When he told me her name I realised this was the Sister from the Citadel Military Hospital for whom I'd had a soft spot whilst I was a patient there. At my very first opportunity I called on her only to find that she had been transferred to the Canal Zone. I was filled with desperation and made every effort to trace her, but all to no avail. In fact, I never saw nor heard from her again. Sheer pressure of work helped to heal a broken heart and as time passed I began to realise that there were other fish in the sea.

Cairo was buzzing with the news that King Farouk who was now eighteen years old, was planning to get married and preparations were already in hand to lighten up the town.

Whereas, throughout the world, and especially in Europe, the situation was looking very grim indeed, with Hitler's Ally just on the other side of a barbed wire fence from where we were training, things really started to happen in Egypt. But the Band still played on: the Officers still played their Polo and the sporting programme was still being carried through to it's seasonal completion.

When I was attached to the 15th/19th Hussars in Shorn-cliffe, some of the old soldiers used to tell me about a woman they all knew in a brothel in Cairo way back in 1929. Tiger Lil was her name. They told me that if I ever got to Cairo to look her up and remember them to her. Well, I did just that when I visited the place for the first time. The first house I went in I disclosed the nature of my business and sure enough they told me where I could find her, so off I went in search of Tiger Lil. I found her without too much difficulty and when I mentioned a few names of the past she invited me in. She was now a rather elderly woman but still full of life. We chatted for some time, mainly her reminiscing about some of the names I had mentioned. We had coffee and then she introduced me to a much younger Italian girl who gave me my first lessons in sex. This was the first of many such lessons sometimes with different teachers. Naturally, the girls called me 'Tich'. The brothels in this part of Cairo were authorised; that is to say they were under strict control of the Army Medical Staff, with periodical medical inspections. When anyone used these facilities he would get a small form on which the name of the girl and the date stamped. Should anyone be unlucky enough to get VD and produce his form, the culprit was easily traced and the necessary action taken. The man would not lose his pay as would be the case if he caught VD outside the authorised establishments.

My intensive training was continuing. I fired my course on the ranges and qualified for my extra pay; just six more points and I would have qualified as a marksman. I enjoyed these days at the Ranges. One day we would be down the 'Butts' marking the targets, another time we would be shooting. This went on for several days. I was in fact adjusting to my new duties very well and was becoming a proper soldier. I had thrown grenades; driven a car; fired both the Rifle and VB machine gun and I was now undergoing a first-aid course; all this as well as music, swimming, boxing and anything relevant to the present time.

In the Squadron boxing I was drawn against a chap from 'B' Squadron nicknamed 'Popeye'. He was a lot taller than I and as I knew had much longer reach, therefore any fears I had were well-grounded. He was no novice, hence his nickname, and I soon found myself on the wrong end of a good and well-placed straight left. Although he didn't have it all his own way, I was easily out-pointed. That was the last time I fought in the ring; not that I was scared but I had at last realised that in view of my size (or rather lack of it) I was never going to meet a man my size, so I decided to 'call it a day'.

Rumours were circulating that the Regiment was to change from light cars to light tanks, so further courses were taken up. These did not affect the Band so our duties carried on as usual. I decided to try my hand at tennis. My very good friend, Taffy Morgan, was already a dab hand at it and agreed to teach me. The courts were of hard sand so the game was pretty fast. I'm not quite sure if he made the rules up as he went along as I never seemed to score any points: whereas, at Badminton, a game I knew very well, I fared better and usually scored more points than Taffy.

Taffy and I would often go to Cairo together where we frequented a certain bar. He would usually get up and play the piano at which he excelled and, like most Welshman, he could also sing with a rich tenor voice. I agreed one night very reluctantly to play a tune on the clarinet (borrowed from one of the quartet who regularly played there) in response to Taffy's request. He suggested the Intermezzo from 'Cavalleria Rusticana' and accompanied me on the piano. To my amazement it went down a treat and at the end we were well applauded by a full house. We often went to that bar and were frequently asked to give them a tune, but I declined, preferring rather to sit and listen; whereas Taffy was in his element playing and singing. Our trips out together tapered off once Taffy started courting an Italian girl, which soon developed into a serious romance. To my mind I didn't like the idea in view of the worsening world situation and I did actually ask him once what would happen to his girl if Italy, being an ally of Germany (in the event of war) was on the opposing side. I think this was a problem he had thought about but he continued the courtship. We had some smashing times but Vimto or lemonade were still the only drinks I would take.

The wedding day of King Farouk arrived in a big way; uncontrollable merriment, I'd call it; some even went quite berserk. In view of this behaviour the troops were instructed to keep a low profile and if going into town to go in pairs. The celebrations carried on for a week. We, the Band had an engagement at Mena near the Pyramids during this period. We travelled in the Regimental bus and nearly had to fight our way through Cairo because of the drink-maddened crowds. We were dressed in summer whites and as we were crawling through the town and approaching the students' area, some silly so-and-so turned a hose on us. Before we could even get the bus windows up, some of us were well and truly soaked. We couldn't do anything about it, although some of the Bandsmen wanted to get out and have a go, but that was out of the question. We arrived at the Mena House Hotel to play at the gymkhana in a pretty soggy state, but were appreciated nevertheless. Our uniforms dried out as we played but it didn't do much for the starch in them. Oh, well, the show must go on! The return trip to Barracks was just as hazardous but this time we kept the windows closed and so arrived, dry and all in one piece.

We all clubbed together to buy a Telefunken Radiogram with a green magic eye for fine tuning. It cost us £30; quite a lot of money for those days. We purchased it mainly to hear and play our recording of 'The Three Bears' which had been a huge success. This we played over and over until everyone was glad that we started a Record Club which was to raise funds to enlarge our variety of records. In a very short space of time we had a good assortment and it was so popular that it was hardly ever off.

Although cocooned in our self-contained existence we couldn't but help notice, through the national press and radio, that the war clouds were gathering and looking very black indeed. In London, the Foreign Secretary, Anthony Eden, had resigned after serious disagreement with the Prime Minister, Neville Chamberlain. The Germans had marched into Austria and the over-all situation warranted a step-up in military preparedness. Our training was accelerated and the building of a Middle East Force was to be created. The Regiment, including the Band, spent more time in the desert that they did in Barracks, and the regimental training took on a very serious role. We were getting accustomed to sleeping on a sandy bed among the creepy crawlies. I had acquired a half empty petrol tin which I kept beside my bed and any unwelcome intruder who dared to call was promptly placed in the tin for future studies. I was no longer frightened of the little beasts but rather enthralled by them and spent countless hours watching their antics. Great respect was necessary with some visitors, such as the black scorpions who had a deadly sting. Not so a three-foot iguana that presented itself one day during a sandstorm. My mate quite expertly lassoed it but not until he had freed it from a vicious grip on his boot with it's teeth. It eventually became a pet but later bit through it's leash to freedom

On these periods away from Barracks food was what you made it. Never was there any fresh meat, always tinned; in fact the rations supplied could become very monotonous: then one day whilst on the move we stopped within sight of a Bedouin camp for a 'brew-up'. I had an idea, which was sparked off when I saw some chickens that belonged to the Bedouins. I could speak Arabic so I suggested to my crew that I go over to see if I could do some business for some fresh meat. Off I went with a sandbag full of goodies, such as tins of 'Meat and Veg' (which by now we were heartily sick of), plus some Army biscuits that we could hardly get our teeth into and some cash that we'd collected from the crew, not forgetting some tea which was very popular with the natives. As I set out I was confident that with this assortment I should be able to secure a satisfactory deal. On approaching the camp the 'piards' (desert dogs) came out to greet me first and with them kicking up a row, the menfolk were quick to follow. I greeted them with an Arabic greeting to which they replied, then I got down to business, but I hadn't taken into account that the Bedouin spoke a completely different dialect. This threw me rather but eventually I was able to communicate sufficiently to make myself understood. Another snag I encountered was that they didn't use money, but they were prepared to barter, with tea high on their shopping list; so I managed to get two good chickens and some eggs for half a pound of tea. For some tinned meats they exchanged a good helping of goat's milk but the biscuits I threw in for good measure, which they thought were paving stones I think!

The crew were delighted with my purchases but were amused by the kiddies that had followed me. We loaded up the vehicle with our produce, the chicken were already crated by the way, gave the kiddies some sweets, which more than likely they had never seen before, and set off to our next destination. This sort of trade became very commonplace on future desert trips and we allowed for this by buying up lots of tea, which was a very cheap commodity. Again, of course, you get the wide boys, who eventually spoil a good thing. The racket was bartering used tea, which had been thoroughly dried, then bagged and resold. It was a good thing we kept on the move as the 'bush' telegraph among the Bedouins was very efficient and it wasn't long before they were demanding sealed and unopened packets.

Thanks to the initiative of one of my mates we finished up with a live goat. 'For fresh milk,' he said in response to the consternation of everyone. Unfortunately, there was quite an art to milking a playful goat, as we were soon to find out so, as you may have guessed, he finished up in the cooking pot and a very tasty meal he made too.

Another means of securing fresh meat was to stalk and shoot gazelles, which sometimes came into view. These animals were residents of the Western desert but seldom showed themselves, so it would be quite an achievement to put venison on the evening menu. To do this we had to improvise our cooking facilities, for the chicken also. Here I learnt to make an 'Aldershot Oven' and to use it to good effect. An empty four-gallon petrol can was ideal for the purpose, after removing both the top and bottom; then with one corner cut down and opened out it would form an arch when placed on the ground. The object then was to cover it completely with a mixture of sand and water to a thickness of about six inches and then left in the hot sun to bake hard. The top of the can was placed as the back and covered and treated likewise and the bottom converted into a front door. A fire was made inside the oven to heat the whole thing to a temperature of about four-hundred degrees, then it was removed and the prepared 'joint' placed in, sealing it airtight with the prepared door. After a period of about two hours, hey, presto! out would come a well-roasted meal – after removing the door, of course.

Another new experience for me on these trips was the relentless sandstorms that would occur from time to time. Oh the frustration of sand getting into everything! We had to get accustomed to eating, drinking and sleeping SAND. If you made a mug of tea, by the time you drank it, it would be half tea and half sand. It was a particular nuisance to our firearms, which simply had to be clean and functional at all times. We would take special precautions on our weaponry in Barracks before ever heading into the desert, which consisted of a light oiling, after a thorough cleaning; then we would have to bandage all the working parts with a special cloth, ensuring that the barrel was well and truly 'bunged up' and all metal parts covered. The rifle would then be placed into a canvas bag, especially designed for the job. Nevertheless, on freeing them from their airtight cocoons one would find that the elements had blown the sand in, which had stuck to the oiled metal parts. So, after normality returned to the desert we would have to set about cleaning our guns again. Another nuisance was the trouble the sand caused to our vehicles in the form of petrol stoppages, which we had to learn to cope with also.

We moved south of Mersa Matruh to a piece of desert named 'Charing Cross'. Here we set up a tented base from which schemes and reccys were dispatched. Those of us who didn't have a tent to sleep in built our own 'Tin Pan Alley'. It was constructed of four gallon petrol tins filled with sand and piled one on top of the other on four sides and about four tins high. This would make a small dwelling for two and when covered with a ground sheet made a weatherproof shelter. This technique was repeated as often as was necessary until everyone was accommodated, a regular miniature 'Tin Pan Alley'.

After a particularly hard day in the field, one evening I set to making myself some pancakes, sometimes called flapjacks by some. I had a frying pan, some lard and plenty of flour, so I built a fire and got cracking. Of course I made some for the crew and as the smell wafted in the desert air a crowd began to form. There were calls of 'Do us one, Tich,' and 'Can I have one?'. One fellow said 'I've got some flour for mine, Tich,' so I made a bargain with them. It was this. If they could catch them from the toss then they could have one. This was great fun and to my surprise not many hit the sand!

Then down came the rain. This really put a damper on things in more ways than one. It lasted for three days non-stop. This was, of course, very unusual and caught us all by surprise, especially the quagmire that ensued; vehicles were bogged down, tents were washed away but my little shack survived. It was still raining when I settled down to sleep. I was rudely awakened by someone throwing a bath of water over me – as I thought. I was drenched and suddenly draped in my ground sheet. It had collapsed with the sheer weight of water and my buddy and I had to set to and clear the mess up. Everybody was at the same task in the pouring rain the following morning. I recovered all my gear and was given permission to put it in the back of a lorry and, as if in compensation, we could sleep there too for the next couple of nights.

So it was a welcome order when it came that we pack up and return to Barracks.

CHAPTER 11

Wars old and new

What a week they had planned for us! Back to Barracks to a good bath and a decent meal (without sand) and then on to Band duties.

Sunday – Church Parade, Monday – RHA Officers' Mess, Tuesday – our own Officers' Mess, Wednesday – rehearsals for the Square Concert on the Thursday, (not forgetting the weekly 'de-bugging'), Friday – a section of the Band formed a small orchestra and were booked to play at the Cairo Opera House. We rounded off the week with the entire Band playing at the Heliopolis Races. Very little time for sport as you can see, particularly as I had a trumpet guard duty to do on Wednesday night. I mounted with the other guards as usual on the Square where we were inspected by the duty Sergeant Major or RSM and then by the Duty Officer. There were two Officers who were delighted to see me on guard. Both were just a little taller than I. I remember one of them telling me 'You are the only person in the Regiment I can inspect properly, I can even inspect your cap badge at close quarters.'

Our swimming team was seriously depleted by men going home, so we weren't doing too well, although their replacements contained a couple of hopefuls. The Water Polo team suffered the most and it was left to us ex-Boys to build a new team; the nucleus consisted of just three of us. My diving was still proving good at this stage but I began to doubt if I would ever get to the Olympics in 1940. Firstly, I was pretty static in my training owing to the pressure of duties which left little time for practice. Secondly, there were the rumblings of war on the European Continent. Our Prime Minister, Neville Chamberlain, was getting into all sorts of trouble. What with Germany marching into Austria, followed by threatening noises against Czechoslovakia, and to everyone's surprise the Sudentenland was taken over without even a shot being fired. I really couldn't see much chance of us returning home either, nor could I see much future for the Band. All too soon, it seemed, that with the Italian troops massing all over Africa (they being an ally of Hitler), indicated trouble for us, particularly as we were so ill-equipped and unprepared, in spite of the warning voices heard hitherto, which had gone unheeded.

To give you some idea just exactly how ill-equipped we really were I must relate that facing the huge Italian Army on the other side of the wire was a pathetic section of the British Army consisting of the Matruh Mobile Force, sadly behind the times with their equipment. For example, the Force consisted of the 8th Hussars with Ford V8 pick-ups; the 7th Hussars with an assortment of light M.K. III and M. IV 6B tanks; the 11th Hussars with 1914-18 Rolls Royce armoured cars with a few Morris Armoured cars; the RTR just out from England with light tanks which were almost worn out; the Royal Artillery with only 3.7 Howitzers; three Infantry Regiments and supporting units. The RAF were in desperate shape too with Gloster Gladiators as front line fighters; the Lysander as a Reccy plane and the Harts as the bombers. This puny Force didn't stand a chance against Mussolini's Modern Army if he had the guts to take us on. In view of this imbalance of the two Armies every effort was made to improve the efficiency of the Mobile Force. Normal duties went beside the board with more and more time spent in the desert training and the Regiment learning to become familiar with the rest of the Mobile Force, which was gradually welding itself into a Mobile Division. This was the beginning, in fact, of the now famous 7th Armoured Division – The Desert Rats.

Came October and the Regiment returned to Cairo. This was not to relax in any way but rather to carry on further intensive training. In England after a third visit by our Prime Minister to the German Chancellor, Adolf Hitler, he returned to London much to the relief of everyone with an assurance from Hitler that he had no further territorial claims on his neighbours. So it was quoted that 'It was peace in our time'. The Generals in our part of the world didn't fall for that so it was 'training as usual'.

In spite of the pressure of duties the Band were still carrying out their normal routine. It was customary to carry on Band practice through the entire morning with a tea-break at about 10.30 a.m. when there would be a mad scramble for the NAAFI to join the queue for tea and cakes. We were expected back promptly to resume Band practice at 11.00 a.m. Because of the rush involved for everyone, this procedure was suspended after the Bandmaster agreed that two of his Bandsmen should prepare the victuals in his house.

This would make for a more leisurely tea break so it was decided that his Batman and another Bandsman should take on this chore. The first day of the new system worked a treat, but the cakes were somewhat on the hard side resembling a solid rock cake. In spite of this, everyone was prepared to make allowances having been spared the rushing and queuing of the old system, and not forgetting that we paid less, too. On the following day, although the brew of tea was good, the rock-hardened cakes seemed to inflame everyone down to the last man. Without warning or premeditation the cakes were hurled back at the two men caterers. Had they not run for it I think they may well have been stoned to death! Its not so surprising that it was back to the old system and the mad rush and scramble.

In my Regimental history studies I had learned about the daring deeds of my Regiment in the epic 'Charge of the Light Brigade' years earlier, and now the film was being shown at the Garrison Cinema; this I had to see, especially as it was only a few days earlier that I had read a true account of the battle written by a trooper who had actually been there. He related it to his father thus:

'It was about nine o'clock and the morning was clear and bright; in fact as beautiful a morning as you would wish to see. We could hear the dull boom of the firing and the shouts of the men, and occasionally when the smoke lifted, saw here and there flying parties of men, but little more, owing to the nature of the ground, and we were chatting together in groups expecting every moment the orders to move – some wondering whether we should have a slap at the Russians or not, and I'm quite sure we all hoped for it. I should say that we had been removed again from the vineyard to the top of the hill, when

we saw our Colonel (Shewell) galloping up to take the command from Major de Salis (who was then in charge) and says to one of our men 'Well, I'm damned, if it isn't the Colonel.' The fact is, we had left him very ill, as we thought, in his tent for he had been sadly troubled with gout and sickness and suffering like the rest of us, besides too old for such exposure. But he was full of pluck and when he heard that fighting was going on he came to us, and we were pleased enough to see him too.

We (the 8th Hussars) now formed the third line and the 11th Hussars and 4th Light Dragoon being second, while the 17th Lancers and 13th Light Dragoons formed the first or front lines. In the front were Lord Lucan and Lord Cardigan chatting together with the staff and mounted trumpeters, when down from the heights before Sebastopol where Lord Raglan's quarters were, there comes Captain Nolan at a furious gallop – what a splendid horseman he was to be sure – and with him was a French Officer. He pulls up in front, asks for Lord Lucan and giving him a piece of paper and pointing past the redoubts towards the Valley, seemed to add some further instructions. Every man of us was ready either in his saddle or standing by his horse.

I now saw the whole Plain and the heights skirting the Valley, covered with Russian Infantry and Cossacks, and their broken horses again gathering behind the battery, and that in front consisting of some six and twenty grim black muzzles pointed at us, which in a moment would be red hot and panting as the throats of famished wolves. We were by this time in motion and Lord Cardigan preparing to act. The trumpet sounded, 'Stand to your horses', then rapidly followed 'Mount', 'Walk' 'Trot', 'Gallop', and again the trumpet finally sounded 'Charge' and we were off.

I had just time to see the effect of the first fire of the Russians. Captain Nolan, who had lifted his hand as I thought in signal, was then close upon us. His hands were outstretched. He seemed to rock and reel in the saddle; out of his breast poured a red streaming tide and he looked as if his chest had been broken in. I saw him no more. The brave – none braver in the army, nor a bolder horseman – was killed.

Down the descending slope, over the ground that seemed ploughed, we went like a rushing hurricane, with Lord Cardigan at our head, and he 'went in' a regular 'buster'. I felt, as I found my horse begin to bound under me, and gripping my sabre, which I had fastened to my wrist with a twisted silk handkerchief – I felt at that moment my blood thicken and crawl, as if my heart grew still and quiet like a lump of stone within me. I was a moment paralysed, but the snorting of the horse, the wild headlong gallop,* the sight of the Russians before us and the first horrible discharge with still horrible effects came upon us, and emptied saddles all about me. I longed to be at the guns. Every man was seized with a cannibal hunger and could have eaten a squadron without salt!

We had passed the first redoubt and across the Woronzov road we pelted like mad. There was now neither time nor opportunity to take notice of anything. The fire and smoke had partly blinded me and the roar had almost stunned me. We were now close upon the battery and the bloody game was beginning, as hand overhead, with a hissing sweep the thirsty sabres came down upon the gunners, who were regularly for it.

The first thing I did when once within the guns and 'following my leader' was to cut off the hand of the Russian gunner. He fell across the gun-carriage glaring savagely, but I cared little for that, and I had seen too much in the first few minutes of the Charge to soften me. Bodies and limbs scattered in fragments, or smashed and kneaded together, and blood splashed right in my face, were no novelty. It was something more than kill or be killed. It was kill whether or not, and anyway, don't mind it, and I didn't.

I now had my hands full of work, I can assure you. A Hussar made a desperate slap at my head, which I parried and with 'cut two' gave him so tremendous a slash that it almost sickened me to look on, quickly as it was done. I now had to wheel to meet a Polish Lancer who was charging full tilt. I bent down slightly in my saddle, received his lance on the back of my sword which passed over my shoulder, at the same instant the point of my weapon, through the mere rush passing each other, entered his breast and went clean through him.

I now heard Colonel Shewell's voice and saw the old man waving his sword on the other side of the guns. We got through the best way we could and formed line, every Russian that was at the guns being cut down and the cavalry that had ventured to come to their aid being driven back, but only to renew the charge.

'Keep together, men' cried the Colonel. Ah! He did show himself a man, ill, laid up as he had been but plucky. 'Keep together,' he said, 'and death or glory but we'll ride them down,' and slap into them we went again, cutting, parrying, slashing right and left, while the Russians in blind fury were killing their own men as well as ours, as if they didn't care who they hit so long as they could at all. Then the trumpeter sounded and 'threes about' was the word, so I knew Lord Cardigan was at hand.

If going in was like charging a legion of devils, getting back was ten times worse. We had already hacked our way through showers of grape and canister. A regular avalanche of cavalry had burst around us, thinking no doubt that where we had got we ought to remain, but we were of a different mind. One thing I'll mention. As we went back, Major de Salis caught up a wounded bandsman and lifted him on to a second charger he had brought with him and bore him safely through the fight; 'wasn't that grand, Sir?'.

I was watching Lieutenant Seager, who was wounded and calling for help – how he did 'slip into them' to be sure – when an infernal smash close by made me shiver and start, and looking down I saw my hand was bleeding and torn. It had been done by a piece of shell that had just burst. I bound my handkerchief about it with my teeth and went galloping on.

I hardly know how we got back to the brow of the hill from which we had started. We got to the top however, in small detachments and at last the commissary served us out some rum, which was a godsend to us wearied, wounded and knocked about as we were. We then formed two divisions and Lord Cardigan rode in front and counted us and made but one hundred and thirty three men out of the six hundred and seven sabres that had gone down with him! So I leave you to guess the slaughter that had been made of us – in the short half-hour all had begun and finished – not to speak of the Russians that lay piled among the guns and on the Plain to the number of two or three thousand, as I heard.

I went on my horse after we were dismissed, down to the hospital at Balaclava, where I had my wound dressed and was very well attended to. Then I was taken to Scutari, where Miss Nightingale – God bless her, I say – was in charge of the hospital. I was invalided back to England, was inspected by Her Majesty, Queen Victoria, and then given my medals, discharge and pension.'

Such a vivid account of an historic battle was sufficient to fire the imagination of any young soldier, so it was that I set off to queue in the hopes of seeing this epic film. Although I was now on Mans' Service, in view of my size I was still able to pass in as a Boy at half-price, as I had legally done for the past four years. Having purchased my ticket, I was proceeding to my seat when I heard one of my mates call out, 'Boy, save me a seat.'

I saw two 'Red-caps' (Military Police) approaching as I turned to answer. To my utter amazement one of them said to me, 'Have you got your pay book on you?'

'Yes,' I said, and produced it.

He read it thoroughly. I could almost feel his brain working out my age, as I waited with baited breath. Mind you, I couldn't have got out of Barracks without having my pay book with me, so it would have been fruitless to have lied; so I was caught red-handed. He escorted me outside and then asked the vital question, 'How old are you?'

Not wanting to exacerbate the situation any further, I replied 'Eighteen, Sir,' (hoping to get away with it).

'Then you will accompany me to the 8th Hussars' Guardroom,' he said.

That was my trip to the Cinema knocked on the head, but I was more concerned now as to what they were going to do with me. I was soon to find out as we entered the Guardroom. The duty NCO listened intently to what was said, gave me a wry smile, then put me behind bars. Charges followed against me of defrauding the Cinema of five akkers each visit over a period of about a year; but apart from the time I was actually caught going in, nobody but me could say just how much I had fiddled. Of course, I said that it had been the first time I'd been to the Cinema in ages. All to no avail. I was up before the Commanding Officer the following morning and my goose was cooked before it started! I was given seven days Jankers and ordered to refund the Cinema the sum of £E3. Imagine my surprise on going to pay the fine to the Cinema Manager when he would only accept half; after all, I was a good customer of his and a friend into the bargain! When he gave me a receipt for £E3, I felt I had been dealt with most liberally, in fact, it was a greater punishment to have been denied the opportunity of seeing such an outstanding historical film. Needless to say, I had learnt my lesson the hard way; never again would I defraud the Cinema, but I searched out my mate and thanked him in no uncertain terms for having landed me in it.

CHAPTER 12

From peace to war

The Regimental Polo Team was doing extraordinarily well during the 1938 season. They had won to date six cups which indeed was a record, but it was tinged with regret in that it was felt that this would be the last season, in view of the gathering crisis in Europe.

Christmas was celebrated by the Regiment in the usual festive manner with the New Year opening under a cloud of foreboding. The war drums in Europe were rising to a crescendo which could be heard in the Middle East; so much so that our training was intensified even further. There was now to be a change-over from Ford V8 vehicles to light tanks which meant the learning of more new skills for many of us. These tanks were 'cast-offs' from the 7th Hussars, but would temporarily fill the gap and would enable us to be an effective part of the newly formed Armoured Brigade.

At this period of time we, the Band, were to undergo our greatest upheaval. We were to become fighting men and were to be formed into an Anti-Tank Troop. We were issued with two-pounder anti-tank guns, mounted on 15-hundredweight trucks (portees). The training was tough and fast, as if every moment counted. It would involve scrambling up and down the portee, adjusting the guns, first up and then down, over and over again, until it was found that we could, in fact, get ourselves into action in a matter of seconds. The fatigue that followed was shattering. Then there were the guns and their capabilities to be learnt with repeated readings of sighting targets etc. all to be done at top speed, until we eventually became a most proficient troop and were to be congratulated by our Commanding Officer. Very encouraging, we felt. We were now ready for all this training to be put to the test, so off we went to the desert.

For this, we were split into groups of four-men crews to each vehicle, consisting of a gun commander, driver, layer and loader, and 'time-clock competitions' held to promote greater efficiency. It was tough but in some strange way we enjoyed it. Ammunition was seriously curtailed with two rounds only being permitted per crew member to fire on the Ranges in view of being in short supply. The Senior Officers watched our progress intently and were highly gratified to see 'that every shot was a hit' on their visit to the Ranges. This encouraged the crews immensely. Our trips out to the desert were now more frequent, with only very short periods in Barracks; in fact, the desert had practically become home! We were feeling more like 'desert rats' than men! Our Troop was now ready to join the Regiment for the regimental schemes and manoeuvres. Our crews had become close-knit groups and I was lucky; my driver knew all the Army desert songs, which he taught me. At the end of the day, when we were too tired to do anything else, we would enjoy a good sing-song.

By March, the world situation had deteriorated even further in that Germany had invaded Czechoslovakia. This latest event sent the diplomatic dignitaries into hectic consultations. Our Government in London recognised this latest act as an infringement of the agreement reached with our Prime Minister in Munich the previous year, which had led everyone to believe that it was 'Peace in our time'. Stern warnings were sent to the German Government that in the event of further expansionist moves (this was with Poland in mind) then we would be compelled to go to their aid.

In view of this latest crisis, less and less time was given to sport and music, with a greater emphasis on physical and military training. Life was becoming very serious and my previous ambitions of a musical career or being selected to swim in the Olympic Games faded into obscurity.

In April, the world was shaken even further when Italy invaded Albania. Two days later the whole army in Egypt was mobilised; the Band handed in their instruments and uniforms. In fact, everything appertaining to the Band was put into cold storage: for how long at this stage, nobody quite knew. This was a savage blow to my musical aspirations but, admittedly, our minds were on other things at that time. The huge Italian military presence on the Egypt/Libyan border, visible to us on our desert manoeuvres, were viewed with suspicion and received closer scrutiny from then on.

Meanwhile, we continued training like mad, the aim now being to weld together the new Division, with special emphasis on patrolling the wire, and reconnaissance work. During the six weeks' duration of this particular scheme, whilst at Mersa Matruh, we were visited by two Royal Navy Destroyers HMS *Glow-worm* and HMS *Griffin*. The former, we had played Polo against in Alex earlier in the year. It was now our turn to entertain them, which we did quite lavishly. A really excellent week-end which helped to break the monotony of life on the desert and relieve the tensions from the ever-worsening world situation. On return to Barracks in May, the Regiment was officially transferred to the newly formed Royal Armoured Corps from the Cavalry of the Line. Our head-dress was now as all tank men wore – the black beret, instead of our cap and side-hat. Back home in England, conscription was now compulsory and throughout Europe and beyond all sorts of alliances were being formed and stances taken up in the event of war. Russia had signed a Non-aggression Pact with Hitler.

The Italians continued to grow in strength on the other side of the wire; a total nearing two hundred and fifteen thousand, whilst we feverishly integrated the reinforcements sent from around the Empire; a Division from India, one from Australia and one from New Zealand. They all had to be trained into the arts and tactics of the Western Desert.

It was during a break from the desert activities that my friend, Taffy, applied for, and got permission to marry his Italian girlfriend. This was normal procedure in the Army in peacetime and seeing that we were not at war, the Colonel could do no other than to consent, in spite of some bad feeling it caused in the Regiment. Taffy was determined to give his close friends a day to remember and splashed out on the very best, with a riotous reception which lasted well into the night, including a tour of all his favourite Cairo nightspots. The party became larger and more hectic as army friends were collected along the way, until ultimately some were to fall beside the way the worse for wear, but Taffy outstripped them all. Came the dawn, he was persuaded to 'call it a day' on the promise that we would resume again at 11.00 a.m. the following morning. Needless to say, the good intentions of the previous night seemed to languish in the daylight of a Sunday morning when I and two other Bandsmen turned up to see the bridal pair. As expected, they were still in bed when we arrived. Her mother made repeated attempts to stir them but to no avail. Eventually, Taffy emerged. With a hasty cleanup and breakfast we were off again to Cairo (without his bride) to carry on where we had left off.

Any hopes of the Band resuming normal duties were soon quelled when the final orders came through for all bandsmen to relinquish their band appointed ranks and be incorporated into the Sabre Squadrons for active service. So the Band officially disbanded and another of my aspirations thwarted. We were delegated around for further training. I was put on a wireless course and also regular guards on petrol dumps and garages, as supplies were built up into a state of preparedness. On my first guard, whilst on sentry duties, my imagination literally went berserk. I saw all sorts of things that were not there; such was the state of nerves that had built up whilst expecting the possibility of a surprise attack. For instance, I watched a bright star for nearly the whole two hours. Had I been Patrick Moore, I could have saved myself a lot of anguish but I was just a young soldier with no knowledge of the heavens, let alone the stars. With my eyes glued to it, I convinced myself that it could even be an Italian parachutist, as it appeared to descend earthwards. Was I glad when my two-hour shift was over and I was relieved. As I left I said to my replacement 'Keep an eye on that,' and somewhat nervously made for the Guardroom. I felt it my duty to report my 'sighting' and heard that they also had eyed it with suspicion for some time, but eventually ascertained it was the Eastern Star! I had also challenged a dog during the same guard period, but soon I was able to discern between the real and the imaginary.

Although I was getting excited about the feverish activities that were going on around me, I was also feeling somewhat apprehensive of what might be in store for me as the Regiment were sent up to the desert again in August, just in case things happened. We were once again camped at Mersah Matruh with the build-up of men and equipment continuing. Our numbers were increasing all the time at a very rapid pace, but the equipment left much to be desired – so out of date – compared to the Modern Army and equipment of the Italians facing us on the other side of the fence. They say, given time, you can get used to anything and I suppose we did just that. We had certainly become accustomed to the continual threat of war and were engrossed in preparations which, by now, seemed almost common-place, normal routine in fact. Precautions were being taken against a surprise attack by the Italians, such as slit-trenches and gun-pits being dug. These chores were very hard on the back and hands, especially if one was using a pick-axe for the first time, as I was. Some of the rocks dug out were just too big for me to lift; that's when the bigger fellows came in handy. These precautions were carried out throughout the desert whenever we stayed long enough to warrant them. On leaving an area all refuse would be thrown into the slit trenches and filled in again, in order to leave the desert as we had found it. There were no prepared latrines on these purely temporary stops. Each man was expected, when the need arose, to go, shovel in hand, away from the camp and downwind preferably, and was to dig an appropriate sized hole and do his business. Toilet paper, under these conditions, was rationed, three sheets of paper per day, per man, (one up, one down, and a shiner).

During my wireless course I also had to learn the Morse Code, which I found extremely easy, possibly because of my musical ear. Morse Code was essential on the desert because it had a much longer range of transmission. The vast distances between Headquarters and the Sabre Squadron's made the Morse Code the only suitable means of communications. It was therefore imperative that those of us who took this course should become very efficient, as any Regiment stands or falls by it's communication system. Three of us ex Band Boys on this course got hold of a 'buzzer' and in our tent we would send paragraphs from books in the Morse Code to each other; one sending, the others reading. In this way we soon learnt to read Morse at a very fast speed. This was a vital quality urgently required by a good wireless man. This method of learning made it enjoyable, as well as profitable, for as we passed our Morse Test, so we acquired more pay.

Also of paramount importance in the desert was the water supply. Before departing from Cairo en route for the desert, each vehicle carried approximately fifty gallons of water in various containers. During previous reccys desert water holes were marked out on the maps and these would be used to replenish if and when necessary. This had to be boiled before use. With this limited supply of water, bathing was ruled out. Our personal hygiene was of secondary importance, so it was that whenever the opportunity arose to bathe in the sea, the whole Regiment on block would 'take to the water'. A special salt water soap was issued for the occasion.

It was also vital when away from the Barracks for any length of time to keep us informed with the latest news, so Headquarters printed their own newspaper called the 'Bagush Bugle'. This would be circulated among the troops giving all the local and world-wide news. It was from this source that we heard of the invasion of Poland by Germany. We realised that this had to be IT. Our Government had informed Hitler earlier that we would go to the aid of the Poles if they were attacked. An ultimatum was given, stating that if the German Forces had not withdrawn by 11.00am on Sunday, September 3rd, then we would officially be at war with Germany. As everyone now knows, this ultimatum was completely ignored, so come September 3rd, 1939 we were at war.

On September 13th, H.M. King Farouk of Egypt visited the Regiment and made a tour of inspection. I don't know whether he realised just how ill-equipped we were against the possibility of the Italians attacking his country.

Fortunately for us, the Italians were holding back. This gave us precious time. It was inevitable they would not stay put for long, but we were as prepared as we could be, with such equipment as we had.

We were literally in a half-and-half state, half tanks and half Ford V8s – and this was our situation when the 'boy soldier' went to war...

CHAPTER 13

War in the desert

After four years of peace-time soldiering in Egypt, during which time I learnt to ride a horse and play a clarinet at the same time; improve my musical abilities; play and succeed in a variety of sports; learn about women, and in general learn to become a good 8th Hussar. I was now about to learn how to do my part in a real war and put into practice many of the skills I learned during the past two years.

Hitler had decided he wanted just a little bit more, but the British Government, along with the French Government did not think he should have it, so they gave him an ultimatum. He refused to accept this, so war it was. Fortunately for us in Egypt, Hitler's mate, Mussolini, couldn't make up his mind, so we were given a little extra time in which to prepare, and much was made of this respite.

The regiment were out in the desert when war was declared. In fact they had left Abbassia's main barracks (their home for the past five years) for good. Training was the order of the day, but things were not too good for the regiment, as they were half equipped with second hand tanks and half Ford V8 pick-ups, making training a little more difficult, and of course the administration of such a hotch potch of vehicles was to say the least, hard going.

So in September '39 my first job was on a petrol lorry in 'C' Squadron. I would ride around in the lorry on top of about 60 crates (each crate contained two 4 gallon cans of petrol), loading and unloading where and when required. This was no easy job, as a crate weighed about ½ cwt, and when one has to unload some 30 or 40 crates, one is pretty well beat by the time the last crate has been got off.

It doesn't take much imagination to realise just how precious and important petrol was to the fighting forces, so, with much foresight, dumps were laid down in the desert before the war. These dumps were so well hidden that men when given map reference to the location of one, as I was on one occasion, often found it almost impossible to find.

On one particular occasion I was given a map reference, and instructed to take three lorries with me and fill up with 60 crates per lorry. I was issued with a compass and a map, so off I set. I took bearings every mile or so, checking the mileage done. This procedure was carried out until we had reached the mileage required. I got out of the lorry and looked around. Nothing but sand rocks and camel brush. The other drivers and their crews got down and started looking around. We searched and searched, but came up with nothing. I didn't want to move the vehicles because I had done the mileage required, I had checked my bearings again and again and I knew I was in the right area. So the search continued. Then one of the other drivers came upon a small piece of wood no bigger than 2" wide and 6" long sticking in the sand on which was written some figures which meant nothing to me, but as it was the only unnatural thing in sight, I suggested we started digging carefully. So without spades, we started removing the top layer of sand to a depth of about a foot around the wood. Somebody shouted 'Eureka', it couldn't have been Archemedes because he wasn't in our Squadron, but we had in fact found our petrol dump.

Now both the crates and the tins in which the petrol was stored were very flimsy and it didn't take much to puncture a hole in the tin, thereby losing much valuable petrol, and we found when loading up, many empty cans, punctured when the lids of the crates had been nailed on. Having completed the task I replaced the piece of wood and made for camp. My first bit of responsibility carried out in good order.

On October 13th, a message from King George VI was read to all ranks as follows:

> 'In all its long and glorious history the British Army has never been called upon to take the field for a cause more just than that which is ours today; it has never entered a campaign in which the issues were greater, or more vital to our race, and, indeed, to all civilisation. I know well that you realise what is at stake, and that, in the struggle which lies ahead, every man in my armies will play his part with gallantry and devotion. It is my earnest prayer that God will have you in His keeping and grant success to your arms'   **George R.I.**

This message was most inspiring, at least to me. I felt very proud to belong to the British Army.

Training was being carried on as in peacetime, but our Colonies were sending help, so our strength in Egypt was increasing. Then, on November 12th, orders came through that the regiment was to return to Cairo. We went back to

Helmieh to complete our complement of tanks. Helmieh was a hutted camp previously occupied by the 11th Hussars. Here the regimental training was carried on. I was put on an advanced wireless course, and passed my driver and operators course, which meant a further 6p per day. Whilst at Helmieh, I obtained some pigeons and I erected a coop outside our barrack room. This gave me a hobby. The sporting scene was in complete chaos, although some sports were played and I often went to Cairo to the skating rinks, and played rink hockey on occasions. Music was nonexistent. I went to Abbassia to the store, found my clarinet and sold it. That was the last time I had anything to do with a career in music which at one time seemed very promising.

In Europe, nobody seemed to want to fight the war we were in. Both sides were sitting behind their fortified lines waiting for the other side to make the first move, and Mussolini was still sitting on the fence.

Christmas '39 came, and with it the usual festivities. My pigeons were multiplying, and my speed at Morse code was increasing. I was now doing much more driving on the various exercises and schemes carried out on the desert near the Mena Pyramids. By April the regiment was almost fully equipped with Mark VI tanks (still sardine cans with bigger guns) carrying out serious exercises and ready for any action they might be called upon to undertake.

The phoney war in Europe was hotting up, the Germans invaded Norway then turned South and started mopping up the rest of Europe, with, I might add, much success. Mussolini decided the right side to be on was Hitler's and he declared war on the Allies. So it is here that our war really starts. France was taking a beating from a very mobile German army, from which we could have taken many tips, but we just did not have the armour.

In Egypt, troops were moved up to the 'wire' in readiness for whatever might happen. Mussolini could muster a pretty big army of about 215,000 men against our paltry force, but that did not stop our Generals from taking the initiative when on June 11th, Italy declared war on Britain and France. Our troops were quick off the mark; in fact we captured Sidi Omar before the 'Ities' knew they were in the war. Three days after that, we captured Fort Capuzzo, then, with a bit of shifting of troops we captured Fort Maddalena. During these actions an Italian General was captured along with many prisoners, and because it was desert we were fighting for, land became very cheap. After these first actions, our small army had a further four thousand square miles of enemy territory to patrol.

On July 8th our regiment were ordered up to the desert from Helmieh, and were in fact to start the shooting war for which we had been trained. I at this time was still in the transport section, keeping the tank troops supplied with fuel, food and water. In view of the vast distances involved, this was no mean task, and at times it also meant having very little sleep.

There were many hazards in the desert apart from the 'Ities'. The heat was at times almost unbearable, then when the sun went down the cold was intense. Flies were a blasted nuisance, sand storms were no help and the 'desert sores' appeared to curse one. Water was a very scarce commodity and our diet of Bully Beef and biscuits over a long period became monotonous. The pre-war idea of bartering with the

Bedouin was no longer possible because they had all been evacuated from the 'sharp end'. Although there were some left behind further back down the line.

The regiment were now taking an active part in patrolling the enemy side of the 'wire'. This meant that they required replenishment but this could only be done after they had settled down for the night. It was then that we, the transport, did our stuff – first find them, then fill them up. All had to be accomplished in the dark. Having seen them topped up for the following days action, we would then go back to our camp and get in a couple of hours sleep. In these early stages we were observed by a couple of Italian Savoya aircraft which would fly over at approximately 11.00 a.m. every day. We nicknamed them 'Caproni Joes'.

Our routine on the desert was becoming regular, although not static. We, the transport troops of the regiment hereinafter called the 'Thin-skins' would follow the fighting troops and camp about ten miles away from them. As soon as we stopped in the leaguer area we would quickly dig out protective slit trenches, then we would dig our gun pit. This was a pit about four feet deep and about eight feet in diameter, into which would be placed a Bren machine gun on an anti aircraft tripod, for use against enemy aircraft. Whenever we stopped for any length of time we always spread out with about 100 yards between vehicles. This was a precaution against attack from the air. The cook's lorry was the centre of the camp. All the Thin-skins were fed from a central point. This was to prove a menace later on when the 'Ities' got to learn of our feeding habits, they would send over a squadron of fighter bombers every lunch and tea time, and bomb and machine gun us just as the queue started to form. However, we were lucky enough to have our very own early warning system in the form of a certain trooper 'Phil'. If one kept one's eye on this trooper Phil, just about lunch time every day you could see him pick up his shovel and some paper and start to amble away from the camp. As soon as he was out of sight the sound of aircraft could be heard, then there was a mad dash for either the AA gun or the slit trench. Then all hell would break loose for about 10 – 15 minutes. When all had quietened down, Phil would saunter back to camp. We soon learnt to keep our eye on Phil and it proved to be very successful over a period. During these raids we very rarely suffered any casualties to men or vehicles thanks to Phil.

Having replenished the tanks, we would have to replenish ourselves. This meant a convoy of some 20 vehicles going some 20 or 30 miles back to where we would contact the Brigade RASC from whom we would load up with all the necessaries. Often on these trips we would be shot up by aircraft, but as we moved in air formation we suffered little damage, however on one trip my vehicle was hit with some 15 bullets, but on this occasion I was carrying water and although we had a few cans punctured, we didn't lose very much.

The war at the sharp end was going well. The 'Ities' were proving easy meat wherever they were contacted, but the stress and strain put on our men and their ancient and worn fighting vehicles was proving rather too much. We had captured so much useless desert, which meant longer lines of communications, more running about and more petrol consumption, that the Generals in charge decided that our territorial gains were of absolutely no use to us at all, apart from the extra petrol used, water needed and wear and tear of the precious fighting vehicles, so they decided to withdraw back to a prepared line on the Egyptian side of the desert. There was of course no rush, no panic and no haste. In fact as we went back we set up dummy camps, guns and vehicles just to fool the 'Ities', and believe me it did fool them. The story that went round was that the 'Ities', having lost contact with our fighting forces, approached the wire with much trepidation. They saw our dummy camps and promptly bombed them, then they shelled them, then after three weeks they 'captured' them. Prior to this the Regiment had several engagements with the enemy in which they came off best, but not without the loss of some men and vehicles.

The summer was at its hottest when the order came to withdraw. We were to go back to Bir el Kanayias* which was south of the defended line of Mersa Matruh.

The whole of the force under General Wavell pulled back to set positions because nearly all of his fighting vehicles were worn out, and in desperate need of maintenance and refitting. Since the 'Ities' joined the fray their casualties had been some 3,500 whilst ours were about 150. During this maintenance period we had the luxury of plenty of fresh water and as the sea at Mersa Matruh was only 10 miles away, bathing parties were arranged.

With the advance of the Italians all sorts of dodges were brought to bear, for instance on one occasion the 8th Hussars tanks were sent out to make tracks in the sand. They made all sorts of figure of eights to impress any snooping aircraft. Dummy tanks were placed at certain strategic positions and dummy guns covered them. This had the desired effect, because the 'Ities' came only as far as Sidi Barrini, then stopped and dug in. This was somewhat of a surprise to our general staff, but no doubt a pleasant one because of the condition of our poor old fighting vehicles.

I was continually on the move during this period. Firstly on replenishment, then running swimming parties to Mersa. I was by now a driver of a 30 cwt lorry, so apart from the various trips, I had to keep my own vehicle up to scratch maintenance wise. Another task was going to the well at Bir Kanayias hauling water. We stayed at this camp for about 6 weeks.

The Italians most advance post was at a place called Maktila, but they laid doggo, and all was quiet. The 11th Hussars had been carrying out a few reconnoitres around the 'Ities', but nothing serious happened until October 1940. It was decided that the Italian camp at Maktila should be destroyed, so a scheme was put forward whereby the Cameron Highlanders supported by the tanks of the 8th Hussars should do the job. So on the 22nd October an evening approach march of about 30 miles was made and all went well, I went with them loaded with petrol, and by late evening when a halt was called for a 'brew-up'. I had to go round filling up the tanks. I had no idea where we were going as the whole plan was supposed to be top secret. The attack was to take place in the dark, so the rest of the march was made in the dark, hazardous, but carried off without incident. The Thin-skins stopped and settled down to sleep, whilst the tanks carried on without the apparent knowledge of the 'Ities', so all was set. This in fact was the first time tanks had been used at night. By 1 o'clock on the morning of the 23rd, which was zero hour, all was ready, then all hell broke loose from the 'Ities' camp. Somebody had snitched and every gun they had was firing full blast. I thanked my lucky stars I wasn't on the receiving end of that lot, but sad to say the Camerons were. I could hear the rattle of machine guns, AA guns and tank guns. Our attack still went in, however without much success owing to the loss of surprise. I could hear that a fierce fight was going on but I didn't know what was happening. Come 6 o'clock and the firing started to die down, but it appears that the main attack failed, and a secondary attack made from the sea was more successful with our tanks giving covering fire where they could. There was chaos in the morning, tanks were returning full of Camerons, and after such a hard night, tea was high on the menu. We eventually returned to Bir Kanayias. Needless to say there was much said about this attack that was openly talked about in the bars of Cairo some three days beforehand. One good thing came from this action was we suffered no casualties, but much was learnt.

Things remained quiet for the rest of October, but by the middle of November we were ordered up to the 'sharp end'. It was whilst we were here that we actually saw our Air Force. Three Gladiators flew overhead en route to the 'Ities' camp at Nibeiwa. Whilst here at the sharp-end our tanks were continually on patrol.

CHAPTER 14

Bartering and Betting

Life on the desert was pretty hard going, I will try and explain. We slept outside on the ground. Before leaving Cairo many of us bought camp beds for extra comfort, but with experience you didn't use the bed to sleep on unless you had some sort of mattress, or enough blankets to sleep on. Without plenty of thickness underneath, sleep was hard to come by as the cold wind would get under the bed and cool things down, so the experienced among us would use the bed as a windbreak, and sleep on the ground, much warmer. At Reveille, whenever that was, we would get up, and according to the water situation, we would share a bowl of water to wash and shave in. The last man in had to scrape a layer of scum off the water. Breakfast for the Thin-skins was from a central cook's lorry, but for the tank crews, each crew had their own rations, and cooked their own meals. Having received our meal we would have to take it back to our own site and eat it, of course it was nearly always cold by the time we sat down, and if there was a sandstorm blowing, as was often the case, then by the time you came to devour it there would be a layer of sand on top. Sitting down at the cook's lorry was out of the question. In case of air raids we had to be dispersed.

Having spent weeks, nay, months on the desert, one's physical condition was not all that it should be through lack of fresh vegetables and meat. Desert sores would break out at the least cut or scratch and would take weeks to heal, especially if the washing facilities were curtailed through lack of water, and personal hygiene had to go by the board. Our toilet was always a worry. Living on hard biscuits and corned beef with a little sand mixed in, it was hardly surprising that one soon became constipated to a very hard degree. Then of course there were the flies, which caused dysentery, so the 'Ities' were in no way our biggest pest. Apart from the aforementioned, we had to cope with all the creepy crawlies of the desert, some of which could be dangerous, such as the scorpion, the black variety being the more potent, snakes, tarantula spiders, centipedes, lizards of varying sizes and of course the Egyptian scarab beetle, in itself harmless.

During the summer the puzzle was to get out of the sun and to find some shade, and contrary to that, in the winter it was finding somewhere to get warm. No matter what time of the year, unless there was fighting or moving, one always went to bed as soon as it was dark, because obviously no lights were allowed. Those of us with lorries had a slight advantage because we could enclose ourselves and with the aid of a storm lantern we could and did stay up for hours playing cards. On occasions we would have visits from the Kumangetet Van or the Naafi Van or even the Salvation Army Van, any one of these would supply for sale such things as cigarettes, beer (except the S.A.) soap, toothpaste, books etc. Whilst on the desert we didn't draw any pay, we would go to our Q.M. lorry and purchase what we required, and the total bill was debited to us in our Part II paybook, so the need of cash didn't occur. It was under these conditions that I first took to drinking beer, water was so short that beer was the only available thirst quencher.

Having done your purchasing through the Q.M., once a month one would sign a credit sheet, showing how much pay you were entitled to, less your purchases. In this way you would keep up to date with your own monies, and under these conditions everybody saved a large proportion of their wages. Thus when it came their turn to go to Cairo for four days leave there was lots of cash. I went on a four days leave with £E200 which I managed to spend. These leaves were permitted to everyone after spending so long in the desert. On arriving in Cairo, one would go straight to town for a bath, a shave, a shampoo and haircut, facial and anything else the barber offered, then off to the nearest military tailor, strip off and buy a complete new outfit, including underclothes. Having completed that lot one felt quite human once more. Now, how best to spend the rest of your cash. Well, I went on leave with three of my mates, so once we were all decently cleaned and clothed, we set forth for the Hotel called 'My House' and purchased two rooms. Then we really got cracking to make up for lost time. The bell boys knew exactly what we wanted, so in a short space of time we were fixed up with girls, food and drink – and so we frittered away our hard earned wages. Here today, where tomorrow?

As usual I had made contact with some Bedouins who were filling up with water at one of the many wells scattered around. I managed to acquire a chicken and some eggs. The chicken was a beautiful white leghorn cock. It appeared that I wasn't the only one in the regiment with a cockbird, as one sultry day I received a challenge from 'A' Squadron to a team cock-fight. They stated the rules so I chose the venue. The team was to consist of 6 birds, no doctoring, no fittings of any sort; so I went round my squadron to others who had birds and got together a team. The idea was to use a gun pit and put two birds in. If they wanted to fight naturally, well and good. If not, the one who ran would be deemed the loser: no coercion was allowed.

So a date and place were fixed. I named my bird 'Oscar'. Needless to say spies were sent out to see what the opposition had to offer. Oscar was fed well on rice and broken army biscuits, the latter to sharpen his beak!

Come the day of the contest I couldn't get very good odds on my bird, although I was prepared to put my shirt on him. I did in fact find a sucker who gave me evens, so we had a bet. 'A' Squadron turned up in two lorries. This was going to be a good night. As we were the hosts we supplied the beer. I kept Oscar under wraps until his turn came, although I knew he had been seen by the opposition M.I.5. My fight was the last fight, and when it came to Oscar to show his paces, we were losing 3-2, so it was all on Oscar. The betting, all night, had been pretty brisk, the bookies were really having a field day, but now they were going to take a beating. So I trotted Oscar out of his wraps, there were gasps from all sides, then came the moment of truth. I won the toss, so Oscar was last in the ring. His opponent was a smallish bird of unknown breed, but he looked well. Then I hung Oscar over the pit for effect and then let him go. A roar went up and the fight of the night was on. Oscar sparred around for a moment then the other bird made a feinting pass at him, without any ado, Oscar made one big jump and was clear of that pit before anyone watching knew what had happened. I lost my money, my purse and my shirt.... but Oscar lost his head the next day!

Back to the real war and forget Oscar, don't ever mention his name again.

THE AUTHOR ACTS AS THE LOADER DURING DESERT GUNNERY PRACTICE.

General Stewart (Honey) Tank.

A tank camouflaged as a truck to fool enemy aircraft.

CHAPTER 15

Convoy duties

Back to the desert and the war, which from the signs, was about to hot up. Summer had eased into Autumn and the season of sandstorms and cold nights. Our troop situation in the desert was slowly improving in numbers, but as much of our replacement tanks had to come through the Mediterranean, and the Italian navy was at large there, much of it was lost, so new tanks were hard to come by. A lot of the reinforcements were now coming via the Cape of Good Hope which meant a much longer trip, so us old desert rats had to try and keep going on the patched up tanks we had started with. The new regiments from England did bring out some new cruiser tanks which to us was a sight for sore eyes.

Come November '40 I spent my 21st birthday in a sand storm of such density that when I left my lorry to go to the cook's wagon for tea, I got lost on my way back, although I had some sightings before I left my lorry, I ended up in another squadron area. You might think I was thick, but not so. I got to one lorry, and he passed me on to the next until I finally reached my own vehicle after about an hour.

Even some of the directions were totally wrong, for instance one chap in 'B' Squadron said 'you see that lorry over there', pointing to a shadow in the sandstorm, 'that is our Q.M., go there and he will point you to 'C' Squadron'. Well, I made straight for that shadow and when I arrived I discovered it was not the Q.M., but the fitters' lorry, the Q.M.'s lorry was in a completely different direction. That's the way it goes. What a birthday, although I did eventually get my birthday cards from home some four days late.

Things were building up on our side, so it was obvious that something was coming off soon. The Wellingtons of the R.A.F. were carrying out sorties over the enemy lines, which was another clue.

Whilst the 'Ities' had been in Egypt they had built an elaborate network of camps, but there appeared to be no system in their layout. When I saw some of their buildings I was amazed how well they had built them from rocks in the desert. By December the 'Ities' had built up a force of some 75,000 troops to face the 7th Armoured Division plus the 4th Indian Division. On December 7th the regiment moved west, and it appeared the whole of the desert army was on the move. As far as the eye could see at every point of the compass, vehicles were moving west, which, continuing in that direction must bring us into contact with the enemy. Then later that night I knew we had started something as there was a helluva din coming from the approximate area of Nibeiwa camp, one of the most forward Italian camps.

In the morning our tanks left us. We (the Thinskins) knew they were going into action. By mid morning the sounds of the battle seemed to be all the way round us. We just sat and listened, then, in late afternoon a selection of vehicles were ordered to a certain map reference, which was the leaguer area for the night. By the time we reached our tanks, it was getting dark. We filled them up with petrol, ammo, food and water and whilst this was going on we were getting the picture of events. It was the next day that we were able to see the effects of what had occurred the day before, the capture of some 14,000 POWs and much equipment. But our best moment was when we went into one of the Italians' camps, which had the appearance of being very hastily vacated. Here we stocked up with tons of spaghetti and tomato puree which we lived on for weeks.

The push still went on and the whole of the B. Echelon (Thinskins) was once again on the move west so that we could keep in contact with the fighting element of the regiment. Every day we heard and saw signs of the collapse of the massive Italian army. Every day we moved farther west. We crossed the wire and still went west. The Italian air force paid us several visits, without much success, and at one time I actually saw a Hurricane fighter bring down a CR42 or whatever. Nearly every evening we would be on the move, replenishing the tanks, and it appeared that every day our journey west was getting greater.

On the 20th December the regiment was set astride the Trigh Capuzzo track, this was the main road to Tobruk. It was here we stayed and enjoyed our Christmas. There was one snag, water. When the 'Ities' retreated they salted and blew all the wells, so our water supplies had to be brought up to us, which meant strict rationing, and I do mean strict. In fact I was nearly shot for infringing the orders. The order was that our 2 gallon water cans were to be treated like gold. It was forbidden to pour water from one to another to avoid spillage.

Well I had one can that was leaking, so I tipped the water from the leaker to a good one, and whilst I was in the act of doing this a certain officer approached, drew his gun and screamed, 'what the hell do you think you are doing, don't you know what you are doing is strictly forbidden?' I didn't spill any water even in view of this tirade, I put both cans down and explained the circumstances, during which time the leaker was leaking. I was eventually given the go ahead.

Water was so rationed that unless you could get extra salted water, washing and shaving were taboo. We even had to make our tea with salt water at times, this was a disgusting mess as the tinned milk always curdled.

Somewhere along the line I had acquired a gramophone and 6 records. These helped to break the monotony, but not for long. I got fed up with Count John McCormack.

We were promised the full Christmas fare, but it didn't arrive. We had to make do with Bully beef and biscuits, 2lb mixed fruit, (ordered from a mate who came back from leave in Cairo in November), 1 bottle stout, all well mixed together, tied in a thoroughly clean tea towel, boiled in water (fresh) for four hours. This was shared between 6 of us who supplied the water. The finished pudding? Well, something different and edible. We did manage to scrounge some custard from the cooks and made it with diluted tin milk, and a little rum added. After the Bully beef stew, the pudding was quite a treat, washed down with Stella beer.

So Christmas was over, and back to the job in hand, the 'Ities'. I must mention here that our cigarettes were rationed, partly through quantity and partly through quality. The brand was RAF; they were wicked. One puff and you couldn't speak for some time, and your sense of taste was gone for days. In fact, we did hear that the manufacturers were put in prison, as it was claimed the tobacco was sweepings from cinemas. So you can see why they were rationed.

By now we had been joined by Australians and New Zealanders; this gave us heart for the forthcoming struggle. Early in January '41, the regiment moved west to face Tobruk. On the 5th January the regiment captured El Adam airfield and having captured it we then occupied it. The echelon stayed at El Adam, and whilst there searched the barracks and workshops for tools and anything of use, we were warned however, that the whole place was booby-trapped. Drawers were wired up to bombs, doors were similarly wired. I climbed into a burnt out CR42 and when I was seated in the cockpit a mate standing on the ground shouted to me, 'Look down' and, looking down I saw I was sitting over a live bomb, and I wasn't sure if it was wired up to anything, so it took me something like an hour to get back onto the ground, carefully watching where I put each foot and each hand. I must have lost a couple of pounds in sweat.

Once again we fed on spaghetti and tomato puree for a while. The Italian Air Force started dropping 'Thermos' bombs. Now these bombs resembled the Thermos flasks, and were dropped at random. Someone finding one of these would automatically pick it up, and it would be fatal. Warnings were quickly circulated throughout the desert force, but still some casualties were recorded through vehicles running over them.

By the 8th January, Tobruk was completely surrounded, and our tanks were probing the defences of that well fortified town. At this stage of the war I had a change of job, I was given a 15cwt truck which belonged to the fitters. It was in fact the 'Fitters' Ferry'. My job now was to carry the Squadron fitter, and his tools and a quantity of spares. When the echelon was on the move, the fitters and myself would travel at the rear picking up any breakdowns or stragglers. Those repairable would be treated, those not treatable would be towed in. This meant many late nights or early mornings. The fitter had the hardest job of all to keep the echelon moving as nearly all the vehicles had been with the regiment since mechanisation in 1935, and were well and truly worn out. Since the army were now using Morrises and Dodges, spares for the Fords were becoming scarce. Many of the springs were home made, and springs were always breaking because of the rough terrain over which they were going. The tanks were falling apart through old age. So you can see that the fitters had one big job on their hands. We were losing far more tanks through collapse than through enemy action.

By the 17th January, rumours were around that the regiment might be returning to Cairo for a refit, then we started handing over the mobile tanks to other regiments. This could only mean one thing: Cairo, here we come. But the remaining tanks formed a composite squadron, and went immediately into action, then parts of the regiment started to move back to Cairo. Tobruk had fallen and the troops were pushing on west. I was running about, being used to carry petrol to the tanks, then some of the tanks I was filling up were handed over to the 3rd Hussars. I picked up as many of the crews as I could carry and made for Bardia. We located a NAAFI dump, and that night eight of us had a really good binge, both food and drink. Baths and shaving and all in all we had a thoroughly enjoyable time until the 'B' Italians bombed us! We didn't get hurt but my truck was hit by shrapnel, although no serious damage was done. Whilst we were in Bardia we met up with two of our officers. They had a drink with us then told us that we were to make our way back to Mena where the regiment were to be camped. So after filling up with petrol and taking 20 gallons on board, filling up with water and food, we set off for Cairo and civilisation.

On 1st February we reached Mena, here we were to settle down whilst the army under General Wavell were pushing on westward. We heard stories that German aircraft had been seen over the battle area. This was an ominous sign although not entirely unexpected. News came through that Benghazi had fallen, and the 7th Armoured Division (The Desert Rats) had been instrumental in its capture. Good news indeed! Here I'll leave the battle area and concentrate on the activities of the 8th Hussars in Cairo.

The next 10 months were going to be a variety of duties. Firstly some men attached to the CMP (Military Police) for duties on the Cairo – Alexandria road. Another group were sent to police the POW's that were streaming out of the desert. Then the whole regiment, less R.H.Q. were sent off to Alexandria for a variety of duties such as POW Camps, escort to ships. I was sent along with five other chaps as AA gunners on board a ship. Lots of groups of six were on similar AA duties. My first trip was on SS *Draco* out of Hull, with a Yorkshire crew. Our duties were to man 2 Hotchkiss machine guns in the fore part of the ship. Our team was self-sufficient.

We had our own food, and were expected to cook it ourselves, but before we sailed, we went to 'Alex'. With several members of the crew and enjoyed a very sociable evening. From then on we were considered part of the crew. We handed over our provisions, and they fed us and looked after us very well. We sailed from 'Alex' for an unknown destination. The journey out was uneventful, although we did man the guns, and, as they were completely new to us, we had to learn all about them. We all learnt how to strip them, and we all fired a strip of ammo. By the time we reached Tobruk, we were all proficient and the crew had more faith in us. In Tobruk Harbour we unloaded our cargo of mostly food and some small arms ammo. During the night we really earned our wages. The 'Ities' and 'Jerries' bombed and machine-gunned us all through the night. I was some four hours at the gun, sometimes firing, sometimes loading, but all the time frightened to death, as those planes were trying to get a bomb down our funnel, at least, that's how it seemed. By morning there were fires at every point of the compass, two ships in the harbour were ablaze, but we got away almost unscathed, there were some bullet holes in the superstructure, whether from the enemy or from our own guns will never be known. Later on in the morning we decided to go ashore to find the town Major and replenish our food stores, and, if possible, get some pay. We located the town Major, and had a pleasant surprise. He was our ex. RSM, Major O'Shaunessy (the RSM who put me in gaol for blowing 'Dismount' instead of 'Reveille' at the married quarters, whilst I was duty trumpeter before the war). He was so pleased to see us and he did us proud with rations, and pay. Of course we had a drink with him and we parted from him well-laden and we wished him the very best of luck in the most trying circumstances. We learned later that, as usual, he carried out his job with the utmost efficiency for which he was awarded the DSO.

On our return to the ship we were received with open arms, because of the food we had been given: here I shall tell of a big fiddle carried on by the 'Wide Boys'. We could only get paid if we were in possession of our Part II paybook. As we were not attached anywhere in particular, we could get money at any transit camp, so certain 'wide boys' obtained 1, sometimes 2 extra paybooks, in different names and numbers. So when they reported to a transit camp, they would give up a bogus paybook, and provided they remembered the name they were using at the time, they could draw money which would not be debited to their account, therefore whilst they were detached from the regiment, they could draw almost as much money as they needed. I could not get a 2nd pay book, so I was not in the swindle.

Back on board, we suffered a very bad night again. The enemy planes were really trying to knock out the harbour and its facilities. They dropped mines in the channels and did no end of damage. Next day we loaded up with POW and pulled out into the harbour, ready for departure the following day. Some of the ships were loading up with captured shells and POW, and it was one of these that struck a mine on its way out. Well, the resulting explosion was terrific. Bodies were flying all over the place. We were some 500 yards from the unfortunate ship, yet a body or two flew over us. As soon as things settled down we set sail, and got out to sea unscathed.

We got back to Alex and then we had two weeks hanging about for another cargo. This time we learnt we were going to travel in convoy, so we knew it wasn't going to be to Tobruk. In fact it was Greece. This was going to be a most interesting trip. We set sail in close convoy, a new experience for me, and what a sight, some 20 transport vessels and three naval escorts. I was as usual on AA duties and was taking my turn of duty. On the second day out I was on the gun, sunbathing, and surveying the scene with an old pair of binoculars. I saw, out on the horizon what appeared like two birds, but their flight seemed to me to be too low and fast, so I shouted up to the bridge, 'skipper, what's that on the horizon?' He produced his telescope, then blasted his siren. We were for it. Those two planes flew low over us, machine gunning as they went. I was firing like mad, then I heard a shrill whistle heading my way, I felt my head and realised I had no tin hat, that whistle was a bomb which missed us by only a few yards! Then one of the escort ships blew his siren, I was still firing at the aircraft which were edging around, then I glanced over the side, and low and behold a submarine had surfaced between us and our neighbour. The escort ships didn't have the answer. I was scared stiff, when the skipper directed my attention to a low flying plane heading directly towards us. I fired and fired, I must have hit him, but he kept coming. That was that, but we didn't get away unscathed, we lost 4 ships. The last we saw was the two destroyers dealing with the submarine, which they got. One aircraft was positively accounted for. I was congratulated by my skipper for my alertness in spotting the aircraft. We sailed on without any more trouble, but we were running short of ammo. One of the ill fated ships carried an 8th Hussar gun crew on board, but although the ship was sunk, they survived.

We sailed on to Pireaus in Greece, then were sent to a tiny port some 20 miles south called Karacas. Here the Greeks were very pleased to see us, in fact the banks specially opened to change our money for us. We then went into the village where we were treated like Royalty. We were fed and given wine (the local brew called Mafradafney). We managed to get some fresh eggs and 6 chickens for our larder. That night the Jerries really let go on Pireaus, we could hear and see the raid. Then there was an almighty explosion. I was told that the Jerries had dropped a mine down the funnel of an ammunition ship, the anchor of which was lifted up and thrown almost into Athens. The military situation in Greece was deteriorating fast, and we were told we might have to wait for the troops and help in the evacuation, but that was not to be. We were sent back to Alex, hot foot. We reported back to the RHQ at Sidi Bishr and thence to Mena, so the regiment were all together for St Patrick's Day. It was on Paddy's Day that we received our Christmas Dinner.

THE AUTHOR, WHILST SERVING WITH THE 'DESERT RATS'.

CHAPTER 16

Into battle at Sidi Rezegh

Training was going on as we had received quite a few recruits, and some 50 tanks. In the desert, since our departure, things had been happening. The Germans had joined the affray under their General Rommel of whom we were to learn a lot about in the coming months. General Wavell's troops had reached Benghazi and run out of puff, his tanks were completely worn out. The only experienced troops were back in Cairo, getting re-equipped. When Rommel advanced on March 1st, it was no wonder he was able to push on, with inexperienced troops facing him with worn out tanks. By 13th April, Tobruk had been surrounded and being as the Germans couldn't get in, they by-passed it and pushed on. There was a ding-dong battle going on, on the border of Egypt and Cyrenaica. Then we stopped the Hun. Things then bogged down to a stalemate, which gave us a chance to re-equip.

The tanks we drew were handed over to the Aussies, so we started anti paratroop patrols, with 15cwt trucks, we learnt to make petrol bombs, and we had bayonet drills; all preparing for the possibility of a German airborne assault as in Greece and Crete. The Generals of high command were being swapped and changed, but that didn't worry me very much as I took my orders from a Lance Corporal, or anyone who had stripes.

On the desert the Germans were proving a different kettle of fish from the Italians, but they didn't have the beatings of the Aussies who were steadfastly holding on to Tobruk against anything the 'Jerries' could throw at them; stout fellows and very gutsy fighters. I felt sorry for those chaps because the German air force was only a few miles away, so the Aussies must have been bombed and strafed every minute of every day and night, what a nightmare.

Our camp at Mena was immediately under the Pyramids, so it came as no surprise that on the early morning PT parades we were told to climb to the top of the biggest, and get back just in time for breakfast. We lived in tents, and it was here that I played a lot of cards, nap, shoot and bridge. I would play for hours on end if I wasn't on any duty. I had a partner, and we would pool our pay and play on different tables. On paydays, the canteen was like a casino, some dozen or more tables, all playing different games. I would sit at a nap table, whilst my mate would play brag. Whoever got broke first would go and see how the other was getting on, and should all be well, make a sub and go on playing. On one occasion I was playing shoot and my partner was at the nap table. By about 3.30pm I was winning something like £15.00; a fortune in those days. My mate came over, skint, so I gave him a fiver to carry on with. By tea time neither of us had sufficient money to get us in to the garrison cinema, which was only a shilling. We did have some good days, so we learnt to take the good with the bad.

Although things were rough on the desert, we were enjoying life back in Cairo almost like peacetime, although we were doing more guards, and patrol duties, but who cares about them when we had our good nights sleep. We could wash, bath and shave in hot water, and after a days work we could enjoy ourselves in the now very familiar bars of Cairo. There was the occasional case of aggro in Cairo when some of the hard cases would get drunk, and pick a fight with anyone of a different regiment, but I would try to avoid such incidents although on one or two occasions I would unwillingly become involved. The regimental headgear was a green and gold side-hat, and the sight of these in Cairo was usually the sign for a fight, but that was the risk of being in a famous cavalry regiment.

Time was passing all too quickly and the Western Desert was beckoning us back home, so it wasn't long before things started moving in that direction.

At sea the Navy had thrashed the Italian Navy at Cape Matapan, which helped to relieve our supply situation, and amid gloom from everywhere else, that news was very welcome. In the desert many nasty lessons were being learnt. First we came to realise that we had no tanks capable of taking on the German tanks, secondly the Germans brought to bear their 88mm anti-aircraft gun as an anti tank gun with devastating effect, so things looked pretty desperate; unless Churchill could come up with something quite new. General Wavell was sent to India, and replaced by General Auchinleck.

The summer of '41 passed fairly quietly in the desert, but for us at Mena things started buzzing. In August we were issued with American light tanks called General Stewarts, which were commonly known as 'Honeys'. Retraining on American guns, tanks and wirelesses was going flat out. Our transport was the American Chevrolet. We had three American Sergeants and a Major attached to us. Everything we had in the regiment was American, and all to be battle tested by us. Everyone in the regiment was pleased that we were going to be a fighting unit again. In September, whilst in training with all this equipment, we were visited by the C in C, General Auchinleck. No doubt he was very pleased to have such a fine regiment so well equipped, about to join his fighting forces badly in need of tanks.

By October 1st the regiment was up to full strength with all new tanks and transport. I was given a Dodge 8cwt and my duties would be a runner for the Adjutant and the Colonel, a scary job for a thinskin. On the 7th October the advance party left for the desert, so we rejoined the fighting war. Almost as soon as we got settled on the desert, we had to camouflage our tanks with sun shields, so as to appear to any nosey aircraft as lorries.

The garrison of Aussies in Tobruk had been relieved. This was done one moonlit night, without much fuss. The tanks were training as part of the 4th Armoured Brigade along with a 3rd and 5th Tank Regiments. The honeys were proving that they were, as light tanks go, pretty efficient. They were fast, they had a 37mm gun in the turret, and they didn't use water, as they had air-cooled aeroplane engines. At first it was thought that the rubber tracks were going to be a nuisance, but as time went on, they proved better than the normal steel ones. So the scene was being set for a real tank battle. The 7th

Armoured Division had been almost fully equipped with tanks and transport vehicles, so they were ready to go.

So on 18th November, 'Operation Crusader' was launched. The intention was to drive both the Germans and Italians out of Egypt, through Cyrenaica on to Tripolitania. But General Rommel, who was in charge of the Axis forces, had other ideas. With our intentions and Rommel's ideas, the scene was set for a really fierce war.

I was a regular runabout at this time carrying messages between 'A' echelon (the fighting vehicles) and 'B' echelon (the transport vehicles). On the morning of the 18th, I watched a sight that could not be repeated for a long time. As the sun rose, the tanks moved out in battle formation, some 75 tanks spread out in perfect formation. I was told to follow on but keep out of trouble if it came. Having gone about a mile, we then joined up with the rest of the 4th Armoured Brigade. What a sight, some 300 tanks, and the desert is a place where one can see it all. Our objectives were the airfields at El Adam (again) and Sidi Rezegh. After refuelling at an advance dump that I helped to build some time before, the regiment moved off, having thrown off their sunshield camouflage. After a very long march of some 70 miles, they leaguered up in battle formation. The next day the 18th, they moved into contact with Rommel's Armour, and using their speed and cavalry know how, had a pretty successful, although tough day. In fact they went right on fighting until it was too dark to see. Now here I give my impression as a bystander with a grandstand view of a tank battle in full spate. I was warned by the C.O. to hang back out of sight, so I kept about a mile behind. Then when the firing started I dropped behind a small hill, got out of my car and crawled up to watch what was going on. I saw the first shots being fired, and where a German MK IV was engaged I was staggered to see our shots bounce off.

The battle raged all day, but the most spectacular sight was just as it was getting dusk. All armoured piercing shots are tracer in order that the gunner may see the fall of his shot as there is no explosion. I watched this 'firework' display until the two sides broke off for the night. I joined the tanks in close leaguer. The thinskins caught up with us, and for the next two or three hours there was feverish activity, cleaning guns, reloading ammo., filling up with petrol and doing what repairs and maintenance necessary, then brewing up and feeding. The crews then got down to sleep, only to be awakened in about four hours. The Jerries were doing the same, but it appears that they didn't object to the use of lights, as I could see some five or six miles away what appeared to be a circus. At first light, 6.00 a.m., the tanks moved forward to the battle area, and everything restarted where it had left off the night before. I had no radio so I was not in touch with the big picture, but I knew the regiment were in trouble. At about 3.00pm they were dive-bombed by Jerry Messerschmidts; this was no air attack, it was pinpointing the regiment for the Jerry tanks. During the next few hours the tanks took a battering from German MK III and IV tanks, which were far superior to the Honeys. The MK IV could knock a Honey out at 1,500 yards, whereas the maximum effective range of the 3.7mm gun of the Honey was 600 yards. Even then, the Jerry armour was thick enough to hold out the 37mm shell. All three Sabre squadrons were committed before the day was out, and I am afraid to say we suffered many casualties in tanks.

That being said, we did stop a German breakthrough and held nearly all our ground. Towards evening, some artillery units were sent in to assist us hold the line, and with great effect secured the line in order that our tanks would not be encircled. During that one-day tank battle the regiment lost 20 tanks but had also accounted for 20 German tanks of superior make.

After dark I could see fires burning all over the battlefield. I was sent on a mission to pick up some wounded tank crews. I was originally with the MO, but he sent me off to a burning tank for a look-see. I then went carefully from one tank to another, but found nobody alive, and I reported back to RHQ having lost the MO, who went in the other direction.

The usual topping up, maintenance and repairs were done followed by a couple of hours kip ready for a recommencement in the morning. We were still hanging on to the Sidi Rezegh airfield, but it appeared that the Jerries wanted it just as much as we did, so they started on us again. The other two tank regiments of our Brigade came to our assistance, and they too got involved with the Jerry tanks. The battle raged all day; some gains, some losses for both sides. It appeared to me to be a battle of attrition, the spoils going to the side with most tanks or most the reserves. Under these conditions the tanks needed topping up with petrol during the day and it was one of my jobs to locate the 'B' Echelon and direct them to the needy tanks. On the morning 21st November, the whole brigade, or what was left of it pushed north and went over the battlefield of the day before.

What they saw was sickening; burnt out tanks, dead bodies, guns and lorries all smashed up. The smell of burning flesh wafted over the area. The regiment was ordered to attack a variety of columns from armoured cars to transport and on one of these missions 'A' Squadron was slaughtered by anti tank guns. There was a huge battle brewing up on the airfield. On the morning of the 22nd, the brigade joined the rest of the 7th Armoured Division to fight it out with the Jerries for possession of the airfield. At 1.20pm the brigade moved onto the airfield and engaged the enemy. The regiment was in reserve, so they stood by and watched a terrific battle. At 5.00pm the regiment was committed and immediately came under heavy fire. When darkness fell, the brigade formed close leaguer with the regiment on the perimeter. In the middle of the night the leaguer was lit up with Verey lights, and then all hell was let loose; whether by design or by accident, a German tank column had run into our leaguer. Eventually, after a terrific close-quarter battle, the leaguer was overcome. From that leaguer, only 4 tanks from the 8th Hussars escaped.

That was the most vicious tank battle to date and goes down in the history books as the Battle for Sidi Rezegh. We now know that the 7th Armoured Division (the Desert Rats) took on the whole might of the German and Italian armies and came out mortally wounded but with colours still flying.

On the 23rd, the only four tanks left in the Regt. were used as bodyguard to a Brigadier, and 'B' Echelon were resting up. I was sent out with a small party to see if some of the tanks were recoverable. Having repaired one, which towed another, we set off for the 'B' Echelon only to find it had moved, we knew not where. Our party of six vehicles gradually, throughout the morning grew and grew. Other stragglers joined up with us and we grew to quite a force but alas no punch, so when Jerry columns were reported, the fastest of the stragglers fled. In the evening we were attacked by six Messerschmidts. We suffered only one casualty, then we pushed on. The trouble we bumped into before we got back to safety is hard to imagine, I was driving here and there as directed, at one time we were travelling with a Jerry column, and thanks to a thick mist that descended, we managed to get away. At this moment, no matter what direction we took, we could not meet up with a friendly face.

We eventually found our 'B' Echelon who had their own stories to tell, about being shelled then chased by Jerry tanks. It was here that we learnt that we only had four tanks left in the regiment. So in 10 days we were reduced from 70 odd brand new Honeys to only 4, but from all accounts we accounted for more than that as well as dozens of transport vehicles.

On the 25th November our column headed by four tanks reached Divisional HQ, where we collected 32 new Honeys, some with crews, so Major Sandbach, who was in command of our column quickly formed a composite force, and off again to meet the Jerries who seemed to be everywhere. Whilst we, the 'B' Echelon were moving about trying to find friends, and trying to keep out of the way of the Jerries, we were collecting stragglers, therefore by the time we reached Divisional HQ, the column was some 500 strong. At this juncture some of the stragglers were put in touch with their own units, others stayed at Div., and Major Sandbach's column of 34 tanks and almost a complete 'B' Echelon, sought and rejoined our own Brigade. We were still picking up some of our tank crews who had been knocked out. Two days after picking up his tanks, Major Sandbach led his squadron in against a pretty big German column consisting of lorries, guns and tanks, and had some pretty good 'shooting' until towards evening they went to the assistance of the 3rd Tank Regiment who were taking on some Jerry M. VIs. A brisk battle ensued during which we lost two tanks, one of which was Major Sandbach's, but we suffered no casualties in men.

For the next few days the 4th Armoured Brigade which included the 8th Hussars kept in close touch with the Jerries and often out gunned, out ranged, gave a marvellous account of themselves and gave as good as they got. Sidi Rezegh was still in friendly hands, held now by the New Zealanders, but on the 29th a large German build up was reported massing to attack the New Zealanders, so the tanks went in to meet this threat and whilst they were doing their stuff, we the 'B' Echelon were getting the hell knocked out of us by Stukas. We had Stukas for breakfast, dinner, and tea. Four lorries were burnt out, but only four men were wounded.

Here I report a piece of luck I had. Some weeks previously I had been on a mission, and I came across a Bren gun standing out in the open. I picked it up, took it back to camp and proceeded to get it back in working condition. My trouble was ammo, because we in the regiment only had American ammo and the Bren gun fired British .303, but with a bit of scrounging here and there, I managed to get plenty of ammo and some spare parts. I used this Bren as my own personal anti-aircraft defence, so on the day we were attacked three times, I was behind my truck firing like mad at the Stukas as they dived on us. At a crucial moment, as a plane was aiming at my car, my gun had a stoppage, so without further ado, I dropped it and dived in the slit trench just as a bomb dropped, covering me with sand and rocks. When I got out of the trench after the Stukas had gone, I saw how close a call I had had. Seven large pieces of shrapnel had ripped through the back of my vehicle; had I remained, they would have got me. The tanks of the Brigade didn't get away Scot-free on that day. Again they prevented a much larger German force taking possession of Sidi Rezegh, but they suffered badly for their efforts so much so that the 4th and the 22nd Armoured Brigades could only muster a depleted Brigade between them. The next day the Stukas fed us again at the same time as yesterday. But at the evening meal they met rather more than they had bargained for. The RAF were there in force and when the Stukas turned up they were quickly dealt with. The RAF accounted for 24 Stukas with only one loss; the pilot came down almost in our leaguer area and was, of course, invited for tea.

THE A.T. GUN TOWED BY PORTEES

THE REGIMENT'S TANKS HEAD INTO THE DESERT.

CHAPTER 17

Knightsbridge to El Alamein

On 1st December the New Zealanders on Sidi Rezegh airfield, after weeks of continual pressure from all sides, were eventually over-run, and the 8th Hussars' tanks were ordered to go to their rescue. On viewing the situation, Major Sandbach realised that the Kiwis were taking one hell of a battering, so he formed up like a squadron of cavalry and went in all guns blazing. He managed to assist the Kiwis to escape, but it was very hard going and unfortunately the Major was wounded in the process. Four days later he died; a wonderful man.

The Battle of Sidi Rezegh was over and the airfield was in enemy hands. That battle was very costly to the 8th Hussars both in men and tanks. The whole of the 7th Armoured Division had taken a battering, in fact from about 700 tanks it could now only muster a small tank force, part of which was the remainder of the 8th Hussars under Major Phillips.

We had a few days break during which time we could wash and shave for the first time in twelve days and very urgently needed maintenance and repairs were carried out. I was driving Major Phillips about when he wasn't in his tank, so I had a pretty busy time. Then on the 7th December,

Major Phillips took his tanks into action again, this time he only had 40 enemy tanks to deal with, and deal with them he did, with no loss to his own small force. Rommel had also suffered greatly; in fact at this stage he decided to pull back some of his forces. Patrols from Tobruk were a bloody nuisance to him, so he decided to reduce his battle line.

On the 9th December we were in pursuit of Rommel, but for the 8th Hussars, this was the end of Operation Crusader, which started on the 18th November. During this period both armies lost nearly all of their tanks. Tank battles were fought with such ferocity that their like was never been seen before or since. On December 15th, the 8th Hussars crossed the wire into Egypt and headed for Cairo once again. On the 19th we reached our new camp at Beni Yusef on the outskirts of Cairo and then started a period of well-earned leave. We spent Christmas here, and away from the desert everyone relaxed for a short time. On the 31st December a memorial service was held in the Cairo Cathedral for the dead and missing of the Regiment.

Rommel was licking his wounds, as was General Auckinleck, so the desert was quiet. Of course it was a coincidence, but every time we left the desert, everybody stopped fighting and waited until we got back.

Meanwhile in the world in general, things had changed. The Japs bombed Pearl Harbour on December 7th, bringing the USA into the war, and on the 11th, Germany declared war on them, giving us a very powerful ally, from whom we were to benefit a great deal. In the Far East we were taking a beating from the Japs, so much so that poor General Auckinleck had to send some of his much needed troops out

East to help out. Malta was taking a hammering from the skies, so was a lot of our shipping in the Mediterranean. Tons of our replacement equipment went to the bottom.

At Beni Yusef, we were gathering strength again. Officers and men were coming in from all over the place. Out of the blue it was decided that we, the 8th Hussars should become an Armoured Car Regiment, so we drew some armoured cars and went flat out training as such, but it wasn't long before someone realised their mistake and we handed the cars over to the South African Armoured Car Unit. After all, we were the most experienced fighting regiment in the Middle East.

Later on in February '42 we really got a boost to our morale. We were going to get the new American heavy tank, 'the General Grant'. Now this tank compared to anything else seen in the desert, was a definite winner. Its armament was a 37mm in the turret and a 75mm in the hull, the latter only had a limited traverse, but compared to the 'peashooters' we had before, we were in with a chance against the German MK III and MK IV. The regiment would be composed of 1 squadron of Honeys (C squadron) and 2 (A & B) of Grants, with H.Q. Squadron an assortment of both. This surely made us a formidable regiment, so it is no wonder that the lads trained like mad in order that they may return to the desert and show Rommel the now familiar green and gold side hat at its best.

I was busy running errands for and with our officer commanding, Major Phillips. Of course my leisure time was spent in Cairo and the girls, or playing cards. I was put on a short refresher course on the new American wireless sets, which didn't take long. At the end of February '42 Lt-Col

Kilkelly rejoined us to take command of the regiment. He immediately appointed me his runner, so my duties were to remain as before the only thinskin in 'A' Echelon, which, was to say the least a bit hairy at times. This was to be borne out in the not too distant future.

The regiment was firing its big guns on exercises and really getting into fighting form once again. We were almost up to battle strength with tanks and men. On March 28th we were visited by His Excellency, Sir Miles Lampson, the British Ambassador. Training was going hard and fast, more men were joining us and by the 1st week of April, we were fighting fit and raring to go. Then came the orders to move up to the desert, so once again the 8th Hussars were going to experiment with new equipment, but this time it promised to be on a par with the enemy. On the 8th April the advance party left to recce a leaguer site near 4th Armoured Brigade. The tanks went on railway flats, whilst the 'B' Echelon went by road, led by Major Sir Edward Malet.

We arrived at our destination on the 13th. The Grants had to have sunshields fitted to hide them from any aerial snoopers, so we were once again facing Rommel. On the 19th we moved into battle positions ready for a push. We were situated on either side of a salt pan, on which I tuned up my engine and I was able to get nearly 60 mph out of it by the time I had finished.

I should like to give you the disposition of the Regiment as I saw it. The big picture was as follows. There was a line of minefields stretching from the sea in the north at Gazala going almost due south to Bir Hakeim. Both sides building up a battle force, we to the east of the minefields and the

Germans to the west. The line was about 40 miles long. The 7th Armoured Division were at the south of this line, with the Free French at Bir Hakeim. The 4th Armoured Brigade part of the 7th Division were guarding the southern sector and the 8th Hussars were the southernmost regiment of that Brigade, almost in reserve if the 8th Army made a central attack through the 'Cauldron'. So whilst we were waiting we were carrying out more exercises. The 8th Hussars layout was as follows. We were astride the salt flats that ran north to south. 'C' Squadron with Honeys were west of the flats, 'B' Squadron with Grants on the flats, 'A' Squadron with Grants on a small escarpment east of the flats. R.H.Q. just north of 'A' Squadron, the 'B' Echelon were some 7 miles to the east. Every Sabre squadron 'A', 'B' & 'C' had its own Officers Mess which was a 3-ton lorry with a superstructure attached. At this time on 26th May that was the situation; the only thinskins up with the tanks were the 4 Officers Mess lorries and myself, CO's runner. That is how we went to bed on the night of the 26th. I was parked by the CO's tank. I slept by one wheel, the Adjutant slept by the other leeward wheel. Some people of the 8th Army blamed us for the fiasco which followed, but what I am telling here is a first hand story, because I was actually involved.

At about 3.30am on the morning of the 27th I was woken by the duty Radio Operator who asked 'Where is the Adjutant?'

'There,' I said pointing to the other sleeping person. He woke the Adjutant and when he had ascertained that he was fully awake, he gave him the following message...

'I have received this message from Brigade HQ. The enemy are advancing in an eastward direction (towards us). All our light armoured cars have reported back to line 'X': the Regiment are to get up, pack up and be prepared to move at first light.'

The Adjutant turned to me and said, 'Did you get that Napier?'.

'Yes, Sir' I said.

'Then go and give that message to the 'A', 'B' and 'C' Squadron leaders, then report back here.

Off I went and within an hour all squadrons were warned. So the Regiment awoke, the only dilemma was the Mess lorries. They hung it out but started packing. 'B' Squadron was a bit slow to move. As nothing else was heard by about 6.30 a.m. the C.O. asked Brigade if there was any further information; getting a negative reply, he asked if we could get breakfast. I was sent round to the Squadrons to tell them that they could get breakfast but do not get too much kit on the ground. At about 7.00 a.m. the C.O. received another message from Brigade. After which he sent 'C' Squadron, who had the Honeys, out to have a look see. They had hardly moved when the Squadron Leader, Major Hackett reported enemy tanks 4000 yards south of his position. Just prior to this I was sent down to 'B' Squadron officers' mess lorry to assist them to pack up and get out of it, then the first shell landed in 'A' Squadron area. Then all hell was let loose. 'B' Squadron's officers' lorry pulled out of it in a hurry without undoing his superstructure, and I made it hot foot back to R.H.Q. The C.O., Lt. Col. Kilkelly said to me, 'Napier, get back to the Echelon', so off I went, shells were falling thick and fast, so I put my foot down, I had to go through 'A' Squadron area as the shortest route between two points.

As I approached 'A' Squadron, I saw a tank get a direct hit, so I said to myself (I had no one with me), 'I'll pick up the crew and get the hell out of here.' I was doing a good speed, but as I approached the tank I saw the crew baling out. I couldn't recognise any of them, and as I drew closer I looked at the tank and I saw to my horror that it had a dirty big Black Cross on it, once again I said to myself 'Jesus Christ, that's a Jerry!' Having gone some 100 yards, I said to myself (I was always talking to myself) 'I could have taken those Jerries prisoner', so like an idiot I turned round and went back into hell… When I got there, I saw our I.O. (Intelligence Officer) trying to get from the only standing prisoner, his regiment, his brigade, the other three prisoners were badly wounded, so I could not be of much assistance as I was on my own. I asked if I could take the walking wounded with me, but I was getting more and more frightened because there was a real tank battle going on around my ears. The I.O. was so long winded without getting anything from the captive that I decided to get going, so off I went heading almost due east, then someone started machine gunning me. I really went, I jumped ditches, scaled hills and dropped down wadis, but I couldn't have cared less, I just went. All the time I was being shot at until I was out of range and hidden behind a sand dune; I still kept going, then I could see in the distance the Echelon, so I felt safe. As I was approaching them, someone started shooting at me from the direction of my Echelon. I started zig-zagging at the same talking to myself, 'Can't they see I'm friendly the silly so and so's'. Then the nearer I approached the thicker came the bullets, so when I found some dead ground into which I could hide I stopped, got out and crawled up to have a look-see. From the distance I was away I couldn't see much wrong or why someone was firing at me, then I saw what appeared to be a Jerry armoured car moving toward the Echelon from the south, this made me think, then I saw one of our 3 ton trucks going like hell heading north kicking up a high dust screen. I checked my position and I reckoned if I headed north west I could catch that lorry, so using the wadi I had stopped in, I set off; when I reckoned I was out of range of the machine gun I went flat out for the lorry, as I caught up with it I recognised our cook. He stopped and we chatted, he told me that the whole of 'B' Echelon had been captured at about 7.30 a.m. I told him the regiment had been hit hard but I didn't know until later just how hard. At the end of that day, as far as I was aware our regimental strength was myself, the cook's lorry, a few Honey tanks and one Grant. Then from Brigade we gradually gathered various escapers, stragglers and tank crews who had managed to get away from the battle; another disaster for my regiment. The battle of 'Knightsbridge' as it was called ebbed to and fro for four days, then, on the fifth day I went back to the battle area with Major Phillips to have a look see and to count the dead and identify bodies. This was a ghastly job, but necessary. I saw many gruesome sights of men I once knew.

The regiment had fought exceedingly well against a much larger force of tanks. They accounted for nearly 40 German tanks and many 88mm guns, for the loss of nearly the whole regiment; but they were neither given adequate information nor sufficient warning in spite of being alerted so early in the morning. The whole of the 7th Armoured Division was involved and some terrific tank battles took place that day with both sides losing many tanks.

Now started a period of re-equipment of both men and tanks, because although we got a bloody nose, we were not counted out; men were coming back to us who had been put in the bag, all with varying escape stories. The C.O. was desperately trying to get some more tanks so that we could avenge our beating. Through his efforts 'C' Squadron was brought up to full strength so the regiment were able to remain in battle. The 'B' Echelon was steadily growing, now it was a matter of following wherever 'C' Squadron went. Major Hackett,* who was severely burnt on the first day, was now evacuated, and his squadron was taken over by Captain Firth. 'C' Squadron was now attached to the 3rd Royal Tank Regiment.

Come June 3rd, what was left of 'A' and 'B' Squadron and 'B' Echelon were ordered to Bardia. On my way to Bardia I came across a Naafi dump about to be blown up by the Royal Engineers, so with a bit of fast-talking, I was allowed to go and get anything I could carry away in four minutes. I managed to get two 1-gallon jars of rum, several tins of crab and about a dozen assorted tins of food. That evening, nearly everyone got drunk on Naafi rum and other spirits. I was not the only one to come across a dump about to be blown up. I, who had never touched spirits before had more than my share, and although I didn't like the stuff, I got well and truly drunk. I was so drunk that I wanted to dive off the cliffs into the sea, (I was the regiment diving champ before the war), but one of my friends held me back and talked me out of it, so I went away to be violently sick.

On the battlefield 'C' Squadron were still battling away and losing tanks, so by the 3rd June they were reduced to 6 tanks. Then came orders that the survivors at Bardia were to go back to the T.D.S. (Tank Delivery Squadron) and collect a squadron of Grants. This made a composite Squadron commanded by Major Harbord, but the jubilation of being a fighting unit again was that the Squadron be split up among other units. This was fought against, but meanwhile those tanks had been withdrawn and others issued, but these were almost unusable, nevertheless, Major Harbord was rushed up to the sharp end with this load of rubbish.

We who were in Bardia were carrying out guard duties, and maintenance to our vehicles, I was used as a run-around, but apart from the occasional Stuka, life wasn't too bad. 'C' Squadron however were still at it, until they were told to hand over their remaining tanks and join us in Bardia. On June 23rd we moved out of Bardia and tagged along with the 7th Motor Brigade, then later on we attached ourselves to the 4th C.L.Y. (City London Yeomanry) with whom our Squadron of Grants under Major Harbord had been fighting. The battle of the Cauldron was not going very well. Both sides were suffering very heavy losses in tanks, and the situation was very fluid. Tobruk fell on the 21st June which was a bad blow, then things started to get worse, we were moving east all the time. On June 15th Major Harbord's squadron joined us. June 22nd was a good day because we drew a full squadron of Honeys from F.T.D.S. Major Hackett had returned from hospital, so he commanded the new 'C' Squadron. Now it was an orderly retreat back, ever backwards. The desert was now becoming so confusing that nobody knew who was who. The Germans were using captured British vehicles, and this added to the confusion. I was now driving Major Phillips around. It was at this time decided that everyone who could make it should head for El Alamein.

Major Hackett was playing havoc with the German patrols he encountered, but he found it difficult to recognise a friendly column from an unfriendly one, because of the use of British vehicles by the Jerries. We in the Echelon were heading for Mersa Matruh, and the situation in the desert was so confusing that at any time we all expected to be surrounded and put in the bag. The desert was one sea, as far as the eye could see, of vehicles moving east. The 8th Army heading for El Alamein with the Jerries keeping pace with them, one could see hundreds of vehicles just as many Jerry as our own, such was the chaos.

On the 26th June our Colonel had secured some tanks, these were Crusaders of which we knew very little, but it was a bargaining point. We were at Garawla, a few miles east of Matruh. Then the C.O. had a bit of luck in that the 4th C.L.Y. had some Honeys which they knew nothing about, so a swap was arranged at 6 o'clock that evening. As the swap was taking place, we were well and truly bombed by Stukas and Messerschmitds, we suffered about 14 casualties during that raid. It was here that I left the regiment for a short while, only to meet up with them in Cairo later.

It had been decided to send Major Phillips for orders. So here I can only tell of our experiences in getting back to Cairo. At about 7.00 p.m. of the 26th June, I was told by

Major Phillips to fill up with petrol, carrying 12 spare gallons, and be prepared to move out at about 7.30. We were going to head in a southerly direction down the Matruh - Siwa track to Division H.Q. I knew this track pretty well from earlier times. So at 7.30. we moved off. We climbed the escarpment just south of Bir Kanayas on and on in the dark until we reached our destination. After about an hour we set off back to the regiment retracing our steps. At about 10.30 we came to the escarpment and I was about to drive down when I saw in the dark what I thought to be a column of vehicles crossing our path from west to east, so I woke Major Phillips up (who as usual had dozed off) and told him. I stopped, and switched off my engine. We both dismounted and crept to the edge of the escarpment to get a better look-see. As we watched in silence we heard shouting. It was a Jerry column. So what to do;'Jumbo' Phillips decided to go back to Division and report what we had seen, in order that the troops to the north should be warned. Having reported to Division H.Q. Jumbo than had a choice of trying to beat that east moving Jerry column, then cut up north and return to the regiment at Garowla, or stay the rest of the night at Division H.Q. and weigh up the situation. In fact the choice was taken out of his hands, because of his information Div. H.Q. decided that their best plan was to get on the move east before they were completely cut off. So we tagged along with Div. on the advice of the G.I.

The next morning whilst with Div. we learnt that the regiment with 10 Div. were practically cut off, and would probably be encircled within the next few hours. We travelled about 20 miles with Div., then at an opportune moment I filled up with petrol, still keeping my 12 gallons in reserve, then Jumbo decided to break away and go it alone, in case he could contact the regiment. We travelled east and occasionally probed north, but every time we approached the tarmac road, the Matruh - Fuka road, we got shot at, whether by the Jerries or our own troops we didn't hang about to find out. Everywhere we went the situation was the same, we didn't dare approach anyone, because there were as many Jerries heading east as there were allies. Jumbo decided we had gone far too far to the east to be of any help to the regiment, so he decided to get back to El Alamein, where the Div., had told us the 8th Army were going to 'stand'. We kept trying to get to the road, but there was so much traffic, jamming the road to a standstill, that we decided to push on and it was just as well we did, because the nearer we got to our goal, the more the Stukas were attacking.

As we approached El Alamein, the traffic was getting thicker and thicker, both on the road and on the desert. Then we came upon a lot of red caps, thence red tape. Because of the chaotic situation behind us, everyone going east behind the El Alamein line had to be vetted carefully, but how after months of fighting, getting knocked out of your tank, not once but two or three times can one possibly carry means of identification with them - this was the position with Major Phillips. We got held up by Red Caps and they let me through because I had my pay book with me, but no matter what Jumbo said, they wouldn't let him through, until we espied some of the 7th Armoured Division H.Q., I went over and found the G.I. who certified Jumbo as a bona fide Major in the 8th Hussars. Off we went towards Alexandria, which we hoped we would make by nightfall, but we did not reckon on the traffic, so that night I cooked a bully stew, had some tinned rice and tinned pears, and bedded out under the stars, but well away from the madding crowds. The next morning we breakfasted on tinned bacon and tomatoes, fried bread, yes, I scrounged a loaf off an R.A.S.C. chap who was a water polo player against whom I had played pre-war. I shall not say anything about some of Jumbo's remarks or observations during our escape, but you can be sure he had a lot to say. However, we did reach Alex., and we went to Sidi Bishr where as far as we knew was an R.A.C. Transit Camp, from whom we hoped to get some news of the Regiment. Our luck was in because we picked up a party of young officers and other ranks who were heading for our regiment. Their instructions were to get to the Polygon Camp in Abbassia, but they were going by train, so we gave 2 officers a lift and made our own way. On reaching the Polygon Camp we found the remnants of the regiment there, and the return of Lt. Col. Goulburn who was now acting as O.C. 8th Hussars in the absence of Lt. Col. Kilkelly. We were welcomed back almost with open arms. Jumbo was happy to be back, and promptly went on leave. I drove him to his house in the country. When I got back to camp Col. Goulburn called me to his H.Q. and appointed me his staff car driver. On the desert the situation was so chaotic that for some time no reliable information was forthcoming, rumours were rife, then on July 2nd we heard from official sources that our C.O. Lt. Col. 'Crash' Kilkelly had been captured whilst attempting to break out of an encirclement at Gerawla.

At the beginning of July the situation in the big picture was that the 8th Army had stopped running at El Alamein, and were forming a defensive line from the coast, south to the Qattara depression, an area of salt marshes and quicksands, impassable even to a camel, so no way could Rommel outflank us. This line was about 35 miles long. The strategic position was definitely in our favour because (a) the line was easy to defend, (b) it was only 50 miles from Alexandria which meant our supply lines were very short, (c) Rommel's supply lines had increased by 500 miles and he was open to all sorts of attack as all his supplies had to come by road. I heard some time later that Rommel only had 12 fighting tanks left by the time he came to a halt at El Alamein. Our 'C' Squadron were very much in, being under command of Major Hackett, and were at this moment at Amyria, after some skilful moves through enemy lines, and some long marches, not unscarred however.

July 8th the regiment H.Q. under Lt. Col. Goulburn was ordered to a small village on the Cairo - Alex. road called Khatatba. On the 12th our C.O. was to send one squadron to the 4th Hussars who like ourselves had taken a hammering. This composite unit was to be known as 4/8 Hussars. That was our position for some while to come.

I was running the C.O. about from conference to conference, but we were now living in a tented camp, so life quietened down for a spell. Then on the 25th July the regiment moved to another camp called Ikinki Marijut. It was here that I am ashamed to say that I decided to desert my regiment and take my home posting which I could claim because of my length of service in Egypt, which was 7 years. I'll give a reason here which I have never voiced before. I felt with my service with the regiment, and the specialist duties I had performed, although not in the tanks, I felt I should have been considered for promotion. When I saw some of the younger soldiers given stripes, who had far less experience than I, I felt it was time I tried somewhere else, so I applied for a home posting, and I was granted it. With reluctance I left my regiment for home via the Suez Canal area. Before I left I was asked by many of my friends, senior N.C.O. and junior ranks, why?? I could never tell them what I have just quoted, but on hindsight, I cannot see why the powers-that-be could not see in me then, what they saw in me later when I was promoted to the rank of S.Q.M.S.

CHAPTER 18

Back to Blighty

Well, I and five other ex-bandsmen left the regiment and we were sent up to Ismaleih on the Suez Canal to await a boat to take us home to England. Here we had what anyone would call a wonderful holiday. We were put in a tented camp with all mod cons only 200 yards from the sea. So long as we kept our tent clean and tidy we were not called upon to perform any duties, so it was swimming and sun bathing for the three weeks we waited. Then we were allotted a passage on H.M.T. *Windsor Castle*. Because of the situation in the Mediterranean, we sailed in open convoy round the Cape. This was to prove an exciting trip. Although in convoy, we didn't see any other ships, that is the meaning of open convoy. Each ship was in radio contact with the others. Because I was an ex trumpeter, I was given the job of ship's bugler, so I was excused all other duties. This I could see was going to be a wonderful journey, my mates were all good nap players, so that is how we spent all of our leisure time. One day out of Durban, our first port of call, we had a submarine alert, I, as ship's bugler, sounded the alert, and made my way up to the bridge awaiting the Captain's orders. We saw plenty of wreckage floating about where obviously someone had come to grief only a few hours before. The sea was pretty rough, I didn't see any sight of the enemy, so after a stand to of about one and a half hours, I was ordered to sound the dismiss. Just as I was about to blow, we hit a huge wave and I was sick. I managed to clean up sufficient to blow the call, then I went down to my mess deck feeling pretty rotten, but it didn't last long and I was playing nap all evening until I sounded lights out.

We reached Durban where we had a marvellous reception from the South Africans. A lady was standing on the quay, singing Land of Hope and Glory and we could hear her long before we pulled alongside. It was a wonderful gesture. We were allowed to go ashore, and here for the first time in what seemed like years, cigarettes and tobacco were not rationed, neither was clothing, so we all bought tins of 50 Players, tins of tobacco, I bought shirts, ties, silk stockings by the dozen pairs, with Christmas at home in mind. We were very well treated by the people of Durban; they invited us into their homes, fed us with food we hadn't seen for a long time, gave us gifts and their generosity was almost overwhelming. So from me, a belated thank-you, people of Durban.

Our next port of call was Cape Town. During this part of the voyage I was getting well and truly suntanned which I had started whilst I was in Egypt. I was very impressed with Table Mountain, which we saw on our approach to Cape Town. On arrival we had as good a reception as we had had in Durban. I was beginning to realise that the exploits of the desert army were worldwide news, and those of us who were still wearing our Desert Rat shoulder flashes were treated almost as heroes. Here again we stocked up with goods that were rationed in

England. When we left Cape Town I had a big kit bag full of cigarettes, tobacco and silk stockings. I hadn't given much thought how I was going to get through Customs when we reached the UK, but I didn't let that worry me yet. All of my mates had a similar amount of fags etc.

We sailed on to Freetown but only for refuelling. We did not go ashore. Then we pulled out for the Atlantic. Our course was undisclosed, so we had no idea where we were going. I did notice that once out at sea, we took a westerly direction. This course was sustained so it appeared we were heading for South America. We hit some rough seas in mid Atlantic, but by now I had my sea legs, so I wasn't sick. We changed course on the fourth day out to a north/westerly, and then we were told we were going to hug the coast of America, but we would not be landing. It was a long trip fraught with danger, and the weather was getting rougher and colder, and, I, as an ex-Desert Rat for 8 years didn't like the cold. We were now sailing on a northerly course, I didn't know where we were, but I knew it could only be two or three days before we reached England. Then we sailed into a fog bank. This was a blessing because we changed course to northeast and within a few hours we turned into the Clyde at Gourock. The Captain told us that where we hit the fog was usually a happy hunting ground for the Luftwaffe, so we made Scotland without incident, but was it cold. The trip down the Clyde was one of the most beautiful sights I'd ever seen. We hove to at Greenock. We stayed on board until the following morning. Then came the ordeal of passing through customs. The Navy disembarked first, we watched from the boat as they went through. Next the R.A.F., we saw one airman going through the mill and it appears that he tried to tell the customs official that he only had one pair of stockings. They wanted to see them just out of curiosity, but our airman started to argue with the official, who promptly told him to tip out his bags, on doing so he revealed cigarettes, tobacco, stockings and all sorts. All of which he was charged duty on. When it came to our turn we five decided to declare the lot, which is exactly what we did. I was first through and when I was asked the question, I told the official everything I had, he then asked if I had any money, I said 'not much', he didn't say anything else but drew crosses on all my kit. We got away Scot-free. We were then put on transport for a transit camp in Glasgow where we were given travel warrants and sent on two weeks leave. I was told that we would receive posting orders whilst on leave.

The train journey to London was for us from the desert quite a change from sand and more sand. I found wartime London quite a strange place and I also had difficulty in getting all my kit moved. I had three kitbags and two suitcases, but the porters came to my assistance. I had about an hour to wait for my connection to Addlestone so I went for a walk around the Waterloo area. The barrage balloons attracted my attention, and the damaged buildings. I came to realise that the Londoners had been taking a hammering. The last lap of my journey through South London really opened my eyes to the bombing they had suffered. The area where I was born, the Elephant and Castle, was completely demolished, and I nearly cried when I saw the devastation. I had forgotten what my home town of Addlestone was like, I didn't know what direction I should take on leaving the station, so with all my kit I decided to get a taxi, which took me to my own door.

The neighbours came out to greet me. My Mum and Dad were so pleased to see me that they wept. After all, it was 8 years since they last saw me and I was only fifteen then. It was hard to realise that I was actually in England and at home with my parents when only two months previously I had been in the desert being chased by Rommel, not knowing whether I should see the day out. Of course my troubles weren't completely over, as the bombers were still in evidence, as I was shortly to see for myself. My younger sister who was working in an aircraft factory in Weybridge came home and was pleased to see me. My brother Don who was married and living at Shepperton drove over to see me and invited me over to dinner on the Sunday. It was like Christmas, friends, relatives and neighbours all turning up to see the warrior home from the war. I was giving them all presents, which they were delighted to receive as they were all on ration in the UK.

Saturday came and my older sister, who was serving in the WAAF, came home on a weekend pass. All in all it was a wonderful homecoming. Friday evening I took the whole family out for a drink at the local pub, The Black Horse, here again I met several people I used to know and I met two of my old school pals. We had a very good night, but on the way home I heard for the first time the air raid sirens. Although we didn't get bombed we could see the flames from some-where further north.

On Sunday, my sister Vera and I cycled over to Shepper-ton for lunch with Don and his wife. Don and I went out for a drink before lunch and he introduced me to some of his workmates and some of his Home Guard colleagues. We were late for lunch, but Joyce, his wife, was very understanding. Later on in the afternoon Vera and I cycled back, and on the way we saw a Buzz bomb. It passed over us then cut out, we saw it come down, and whilst we were cycling on we saw where it dropped in an open field, causing no damage or harm.

I always felt jealous of my brother because he was in a reserved occupation therefore he never left home all through the war, and he was in the Home Guard, in which he got a commission. If he thought I was going to give him a salute, he had another think coming.

My posting orders came through telling me to report to the 154 Regt. (9th Battalion North Staffordshire Regt.) at Northants on the conclusion of my leave. I was seeing England at war; the blackouts, the shaded headlights of cars, the rationing of food and clothing and other restrictions. Don was doing some joinery in London in his spare time at some of the theatres. So one evening he took me to see a show at one of these. Ann Ziegler and Webster Booth were the stars and when the show was over, we went back stage to meet the artists.

My two weeks leave was soon over, so I started my journey to Northants. When I arrived, I found Spike, the lad I had joined up with, had joined the same unit. The 154 R.A.C. was a comparatively new regiment; they were originally a TA Infantry Regiment, then the WO decided to turn them into an RAC unit, and I was sent to them as an instructor. It wasn't long before I was given my first stripe. I was instructing gunnery and I found it was a job I enjoyed. After three months trial I was promoted to Corporal with 2 stripes. I had another leave at Christmas. I managed to wangle some extra clothing coupons and ration coupons, but I was still surprised at the quality of Christmas in wartime. We had a Christmas dinner as good as any in peacetime.

THE NEWLYWEDS – MARRIED IN AUGUST 1943.

CHAPTER 19

Training for D-Day

The war in the desert was going very well after the breakout from El Alamein and Rommel was getting a beating from which he would never recover. For the third time, the 8th Army was in Benghazi, but this time they were not going to be pushed out. This was indeed a boost to the Allies, because all the news coming from the Far East was sickening. Capital naval battleships were getting sunk by the Japs. Malaya was getting inundated with Japs, and the Yellow Peril was threatening Singapore. One very bright spot was the fact that the Yanks were 'In' on our side and were supplying us with tanks, the like of which we had never seen before, although we had used their Grants on the desert, but these had too many disadvantages. The sight of the Sherman tank was another thing. I saw one whilst I underwent a gunnery course at Lulworth in the spring of '43. I was on a 6 pounder Instructor's course. Having successfully completed this course I returned to Northants and was instructing as well as the 6 pounder, the Bren LMG and the Sten gun. Then rumours started that the 154 Regiment was to be disbanded to re-enforce the other regiments of the R.A.C. who were short of men, it was rumoured that I may be sent to Lulworth as an instructor as I got excellent marks on my course. Here I visualised an easy base job after the desert. Just sit the rest of the war out on a staff job in the gunnery school. I thought my luck had changed – the shock was yet to come.

Groups of men were being sent to various regiments. Then came the news that I was to take a party of forty men to join the 13/18 Royal Hussars (QMO) who were stationed at Wickham Market, Suffolk. The cruellest knock was that I had to drop my 2 stripes, as I was two weeks short of becoming war substantive. This was a rule that until one had held a full rank for three months, one was only acting rank, and a transfer from one regiment to another unless the rank held was a substantive, the rank was automatically dropped. So I had to start again. In May '43 I reported to the 13/18th Hussars at Wickham Market. I was interviewed by first the Squadron Leader, Major Cordy-Simpson, who having read my records decided I was a well trained soldier, and as he said 'I've got just the job for you', he went on 'as our Post Corporal is away at present you can carry on his job for the time being with the rank of Lance Corporal' (one stripe). It was a start, but what a comedown for a qualified gunnery instructor, Class II radio operator and driver. So I started my new job.

This entailed gathering the mail from the four squadrons, bag it up and taking it into Wickham Market and collecting the mail for the Regiment, sorting it and distributing it to the squadrons. For this job I had my own 15 cwt truck. This was a snip of a job, until one day I came unstuck, as you will see through no fault of mine, unless of course you view the situation with the eyes of our Commanding Officer.

When a parcel was given to me as post Corporal, I would accept it, with the postage money and take it to the Post Office, or to the Railway Station as was requested on this particular occasion. The cook Corporal of 'B' Squadron gave me a parcel and requested it go by rail. He had obviously done this before, as he gave me the correct postage money. I had collected the regimental post and as I was about to leave, when the R.S.M. Duffy Hind asked for a lift into town. He jumped in the back of my truck and off I went, first stop Post Office, delivered and collected. Next stop Railway Station. When I went round the back the R.S.M. asked 'whose is that parcel?'

'Corporal 'B' Sir' I replied. 'What's in it?' he asked. 'I don't know' answered I. 'Corporal 'B', isn't he the cook Corporal of 'B' Squadron?' he asked. 'Yes sir.'

He paused, then, 'take it and me back to camp.' On arrival back at the camp he instructed me to stop outside the Orderly Room, he sent for the N.C.O. concerned and when he arrived he asked the Adjutant to come out and witness the opening of the parcel. On the answer in the affirmative to the question "Is that your parcel?" he then ordered the Corporal to open the same. On doing so, all was revealed. Tea, sugar, butter, lard, tinned meat etc., all rationed goods, all stolen from the cookhouse. He inevitably was charged with theft, but the not so inevitable, I was charged with aiding and abetting. Well you could have knocked me down with the proverbial feather. I carried out my post duties, then on the following morning, I was up before the Squadron Leader, who felt the charge was too grave for him to deal with, so I was remanded for the Commanding Officer. All the time I was thinking, 'what the hell have I done to warrant such treatment?' I thought there must be some conspiracy against me, as I couldn't see that I had committed any crime. The C.O. gave me a right dressing down. 'Your first duty as a cavalrymen is to be inquisitive, you should have asked what was in the parcel.'

'If I had done so, what answer would I have got? My dirty washing.' I was reprimanded which didn't help me make a name for myself in my new regiment. The post Corporal returned from leave and I handed over to him. The cook Corporal went on to a court martial and was stripped and given 28 days in the 'Glasshouse' (Aldershot Detention Centre).

The Squadron Leader sent for me and told me I could keep my stripe and he promptly sent me on an upgrading Wireless Course at Bovington in Dorset. Here I was brought up to date with the latest wireless sets (American), increased my Morse speed, which had got rather rusty since the days of the desert and on my return to the Regiment I learned the truth. Instead of sitting out the rest of the war in some easy base job I had been posted to a regiment specially selected for a specialist job on D-Day. Right up to my neck in it again! This job was to swim their tanks on to the beaches on D-Day before anyone else got there by sea. I started out as a gunnery instructor on the six-pounder as used on the 'Valentine tank'. This tank was used for the initial training for DD, which stands for Duplex Drive, which meant that the tank had two small propellers at the back giving it propulsion in water and therefore the tracks and propellers were being driven at the same moment. This innovation was so secret that even today nobody knows about it, but its invention at the time was probably a main factor which helped us succeed on D-Day.

The tank used on D-Day was the Sherman, an ordinary fighting tank with a few extras such as; a canvas screen or bag was attached all around the tank. This screen was inflatable and when inflated (by compressed air bottles controlled by the Crew Commander on the tank) made the tank buoyant, providing it had been thoroughly waterproofed. This in itself was an art to be learnt, not a very easy job with pounds of black Bostick, but very essential. This waterproofing had to be carried out not only by the swimmers but also by the waders, those tanks which dropped off on the beach, or as near as possible, to a maximum of six feet in depth of water. Thus with buoyancy and two propellers for drive, we had a swimming or amphibious tank. Sounds easy maybe, but to use these tanks as intended meant months of very hard training in all sorts of seas with different currents and tides, and so we went to training.

Meanwhile, in August 1943 I went on leave and I got married to a girl I had known at school. Picture it! Our honeymoon was spent at Staines in a friend's house which backed on to the Thames. They had a punt and about 8 p.m. on our wedding night they invited us to a trip up-river to meet some of their friends. The night was warm and gentle and the river was peaceful and lovely. On and on we went, stopping here for a chat, stopping there for a drink. Time was passing. I kept jumping in for a dip to cool me down, but still they went on oblivious of the fact that my wife and I were just married and miles from home. It was getting dark and still we sailed on. I was dipping more often. Eventually, we turned for home and it was about 2 a.m. by the time we reached their home. Our hosts then asked us if we wanted any supper or would rather go to bed. I don't know if they thought us rude the speed with which we shot up those stairs!

Back at the camp at Wickham, which was tented, the facilities for off-duty times were very limited. I would often go with a pal on his cycle cross-bar into Wickham Market. Once we really got down to training the need to go out gradually disappeared; then it was back to the card table using paraffin lamps, but usually one was too pooped for much else. I was in R.H.Q. Squadron, so it came as no surprise that I did a variety of tasks. The Regiment was getting equipment and one main exercise was in the use of the Davis escape apparatus, which would enable the crew to escape should the tank drown; a very necessary piece of equipment. Troops were now going to various seaside places learning all about currents, waves and wind and everything appertaining to their new task.

There were many curious devices thought up during the war and the tank was just the ideal vehicle. The 'Flail' was a tank with a huge drum in front onto which were attached several long chains and when the drum was rotated the chains thrashed the ground in front, exploding any mines in its path and clearing a track though a minefield. The 'Bridge Layer' was a tank carrying a bridge big enough to span a tank trap or ditch. There were other monsters which we were to see in action in the near future, especially the 'Flame Thrower'.

December 1943, the Regiment split up. The 2 D.D. Squadrons went to Gosport for training at sea; these were A and B Squadrons, whilst C and R.H.Q. went to Hoddon Castle in Dumfriesshire. I, of course, went to Scotland. At this time I was driving the Second in command around in a staff car. It was work and more work, but we did have a pretty good Christmas. Some of the troops went home but I wasn't lucky. However, the Naafi girls did us proud and on New Year's Eve some of us from the Corporals Mess went on First Footing with the girls who were all local. I'd often heard about the Scottish tradition on Hogmanay but now I was to know what it was all about. We had a wonderful time thanks to the Jocks. I gather the two squadrons at Gosport were not so lucky as their programme depended entirely on the weather conditions so they didn't have much of a Christmas. Their training was proving very useful. They were loading on to LCTs and launching in the Solent, then swimming ashore.

Early in January 1944, A and B Squadrons joined us in Scotland, then we all moved further North to colder climes to Fort George in Invernesshire. Here, the D.D. tanks were trying out the tides and winds of the Moray Firth. I was now driving the Commanding Officer in his staff car and considering all the 'Brass' that were interested in the efforts of the Regiment, I was kept very busy. We were visited by the top brass of the Army, the Navy and the American Army; there was very little time for leisure.

The Barracks were quite a novelty to me as I hadn't slept in barracks since before the war, at Abbassia in Cairo, and considering the low temperatures outside it was a pleasure to go to a well heated barrack room when day was done. All through the winter of '43/'44 the Regiment was carrying out exercises on a full scale. Even the language changed, instead of the normal tank language of 'Left Stick', or 'Right Stick', it was 'Port helm', 'Amid-ships', etc.

During an exercise in March we suffered a most unfortunate accident. The D.D. tanks were swimming in the Moray Firth when the wind came up and the waves swamped two tanks, which sank. The crews, less one Corporal, were saved. There was obviously a maximum height of wave the tanks could take and here we soon learnt what that was. Much that was unknown about this hazardous task was learnt during these very vital exercises and schemes, and so it was we were really getting ready for D-Day.

I went on leave early in April and whilst on leave I was talked into speaking to the Cadet Force by my brother, but I had never spoken in public before so I got the kids asking questions which I then did my best to answer. It made a change for them and I did my best to give them a good laugh. The day before I was due to report back to Fort George (a Saturday) I received a telegram from the Regiment telling me to report back to Petworth in Sussex, so I went to the station at Shepperton having said my goodbyes to my brother with whom I was staying. When I got to the station I was informed that there were no trains to Petworth until the Monday; this meant that I was going to be late reporting in, so I sent a telegram to the Regiment informing them of the situation. I also got the Station Master to sign my pass with the time I first reported to him. This would cover me – or so I thought. When I arrived at Petworth on the Monday afternoon I was promptly put on a charge for being absent without leave, from midnight Sunday until 2.30 p.m. Monday. This, I thought, is ridiculous. They had received my telegram, but someone in the Orderly Room had forgotten to inform my Squadron. I will admit that the Regiment was in some chaos with the move barely completed and only RHQ and C Squadrons at Petworth. The other two Sabre Squadrons went on to Gosport where they hoped to get their DD Shermans. From here I was sent on a conversion course to the 75mm gun as in the Sherman. It was a short sharp course at Lulworth. On my return to the Regiment I was transferred to C Squadron, thence to become gunner in the Second I/C's tank. Now, after all this time among tanks, I was really going to earn my bread and butter. I soon adapted to the ways of a tank crewman but I wasn't relishing what lay ahead. I felt they must have been saving up the 'Big One' for me. I knew our roll on D.D. was going to be a sticky one so I wasn't looking forward to it.

My crew: Captain Wardlaw, Sergeant Wright, Signal Sergeant, myself, Gunner, Tpt Calvert, Co-Driver and Tpt Read as Driver. There were to be some changes in the not too distant future.

The hive was really buzzing with activity; intensive training on the new equipment, practice loading and unloading on and off LCTs and exercises of movement to and from Portsmouth. All through April and May the pace was getting faster and faster, so although we hadn't been officially told we knew that D-Day could not be far away, especially as whilst we moved around one could not but notice the huge build-up of troops. Of course, everywhere the DD tanks went by rail they were put under wraps as so far they were still very secret.

On 22nd March, His Majesty the King visited us, then a few days later General Eisenhower paid us a visit. Time was running out. We moved to the marshalling area where we were wired in with nothing to do but play cards and I went to a concert in the evening and, lo and behold, the chap running the concert was an old mate of mine from our days in the 8th Hussars Band before the war, one Jasper Cotton. Whilst we were waiting I played a lot of cards and on one particular Friday I drew my pay and immediately went to the shoot card game. For a long time I was winning. Men were coming in with their wages and leaving broke. At one time I was winning £75, but before I went to bed I, too, was broke.

Then it was all aboard the LCTs.

CHAPTER 20

The longest day and beyond

The date was 3rd June 1944. When we pulled away from the docks the weather turned sour and the sea got rough. Space on the LCT was limited so we spent most of our time putting the final touches to the explosive charges which were set to blow off the waterproofing. An innovation, which I think would have been useful on the desert, were the self-heating tin's of soup and cocoa; just remove a small central lid, light the fuse and within a few minutes the tin became so hot you couldn't hold it. No fire, no light and no bother.

I was feeling seasick by nightfall, but looking over the side of the LCT I could see a terrific build up of thousands of ships of all sorts; LCTs, LCIs, Cruisers, Destroyers, Rocket Ships, you name it, it was there all waiting at the starting gate for the tape to go up.

The next day, the 4th, the weather closed in on us so the chances of setting sail that evening were nil, in fact, we were due to set sail that night but the start date was put back twenty-four hours. Against all orders, I had managed to smuggle a small camera on my tank with which I had hoped to get some snaps of the invasion fleet.

On June 5th we set sail in the evening; the weather was still rough, too rough in fact for the DD tanks, as the waves were much too high, but we sailed on. When we awoke on the morning of the 6th we were still sailing and the sight around us was unbelievable. I did manage to take a few snaps and then the battleships opened up. I knew that what I was witnessing would never be seen again; the sight was awe-inspiring. The rocket ships opened up. Spitfires and Hurricanes were buzzing about like a swarm of bees. The noise was now building to a deafening crescendo. I was in a wader LCT. We hadn't seen our 2 DD Squadrons for some days now, but we knew they were somewhere in the lead ahead of us. I was feeling very excited with all that was going on around us.

Excited? I think it was probably fear, knowing what we were going into in about an hour's time. Then I could see the coast of France.

The stuff that was falling on that coast was a booster for us who were about to land. The bombers were bombing, fighters were machine gunning, naval ships were bombarding and rocket ships were throwing fireworks at anyone who dared watch from the shore. I thought that nothing could possibly live within a mile of those beaches after the pounding they were taking, so I thought we might be in for an easy time.

As we got nearer the beach so all of us tank crews made the last minute checks and settled down in our tank for what may come. I, as a gunner, was hidden away in the turret with the only vision through my periscope. Then came the sound of the ramps being lowered and I knew this was IT. The din around us was deafening.

'Driver, start up!'

Then we moved slowly forward. The angle of the tank changed and I knew we were going down the ramp: a slight splash, a bit of a bump and we were on the bottom but still moving forward. All I could see were two white buildings in front of us, which were burning. Then the angle changed and I knew we were going up out of the sea and onto the beach. We had gone but a few yards when suddenly a terrific bang, dust everywhere. 'God,' I thought, 'we've been hit already.'

I looked around the gun and everybody seemed alright, then I realised the bang was caused by the explosive being fired to remove the waterproofing from around the turret and the guns. Relief! Relief! We were still moving and were still O.K. I could see no targets and none were given me by the Tank Commander.

We got safely off the beach and nobody took a shot at us. I was beginning to relax. I couldn't see much through my periscope and then I caught sight of one of our DD tanks looking the worse for wear. Apparently, it had been run down by a landing craft that had been hit by enemy fire. The landing of the DD tanks was better than expected in view of the rough seas but there were casualties.

Having moved from the beach we moved inland and at last we stopped and the crew were able to dismount. I had a look at France from close quarters and it didn't look too bad, then a blasted sniper opened up on us from a window of a house some distance off. We all jumped into our tanks or put the tank between us and the sniper. Someone had a go at the so-and-so with a machine gun and whether he got him or not I don't know, but he didn't show his hand again.

Here we met up with our Infantry friends and plans were laid for our first objective. All our objectives were given the name of cars as code names; for instance, our first objective was Morris, which we took with the Infantry with very little trouble. A few prisoners were taken. On to our next objective, Hillman: this proved a more troublesome task. All I could see was what appeared a grassy hill, but when the Infantry advanced up the hill, machine guns opened up on them from the hillside. They withdrew. Then I went into action, firing at the position where I saw flashes coming from the hillside: two or three other tanks were doing the same and it wasn't long before we ceased firing and the Infantry went in again, this time with more success. One tank on my right was approaching the hill when the ground beneath it suddenly gave way. They had run on to the Jerry underground lavatories. For a while we were winkling out the Jerries entrenched around the hill then late afternoon all fell quiet and our second objective had been captured. We were then sent off to replenish and we landed in an orchard. Here we made ourselves a cup of tea, which was very welcome.

Early evening and we watched hundreds of planes dropping supplies to the 6th Airborne troops who had been dropped the night before. Then at about seven o'clock we were sent out to take up positions for a reported counter attack. We stayed in these positions until about midnight. During this wait we were able to brew up tea in the turret and feed off our rations. We were told to retire to the orchard and stand down. As soon as we arrived it was gun cleaning, checking ammo and petrol, then a couple of hours sleep.

For that first day – D-Day – our casualties were 12 dead and 12 wounded, but we inflicted far worse on the Jerries apart from the fact that we had landed on French soil and we were not going to be pushed off. All the time more and more troops were pouring on to the beaches. D-Day over and not as bad as I had expected, but I knew there was worse to come.

D plus one saw us up early in the morning and back to the place we had captured the day before, Morris. We met up with the paratroops of the 6th Airborne and off to guard the bridges over the Orne, captured by the paras who were expecting a counter attack by Jerry tanks. This was really exciting, meeting up with Jerry tanks and us in good positions to really have a go at them. However, nothing came of the counter attack but the paratroops were so pleased to see us. We pulled out to the Harbour area when it got dark to do the usual gun cleaning and topping up and grab what sleep we could, but a sniper fired a shot into the harbour area, or so it was said; someone in a tank said he saw the flash of a rifle and returned the fire; someone else saw his flash of a rifle and fired at it and so it went until we had a pitched battle going on all round the area. The SSM blew a whistle and firing ceased. Maybe there was a sniper, maybe not, but fortunately there were no casualties. Such were the taut nerves of everybody in these early days.

Slowly but surely we were establishing ourselves in Normandy. Every day a little bit further on to our final goal, meeting trouble when it came, suffering casualties but inflicting far worse. On the 9th June, D+3, we were given a short break. We had three days doing maintenance and repairs. During this time replacement tanks arrived to make up the losses of DD tanks lost on D-Day. Small actions were going on around us, in which the Regiment was involved, then, tragically, on the 12th June our Commanding Officer, Lt Colonel Harrap, was killed by machine gun fire whilst he was in his jeep. He had been responsible for the success of the Regiment, especially in training for its role on D-Day as a DD regiment, the only regiment successful with DD on D-Day.

Time was dragging on. Lots of time was spent in positions just waiting for hours. We often got heavily 'stonked' (shelled and mortared) but when the shell or mortars started coming over we all jumped into our tanks, closed down and waited for the shelling to stop. We suffered few casualties.

June 23rd was a special day. In the early morning the Infantry had had a hard time, losing many men. Then it was learnt that a German tank column was approaching our area so the whole regiment went into hiding, waiting for this column which had to pass in front of us in open country. My officer dismounted and scaled a rather tall tree from which position he had a good view of the approaching tanks. He was connected by field telephone to a wireless jeep, so he gave a running commentary of the state of affairs. Some 40-odd vehicles were passing right across our front, then at a convenient moment everyone let loose. The din was terrific. I reckoned I fired 10 rounds and I claimed one definitely knocked out and perhaps four hits on others. The column soon split up but not before it had suffered greatly. When we had finished with them the rocket firing Typhoon aircraft had a go at them, inflicting further damage. During these days of battle their most feared weapon was the same 88mm which I had heard of in the Western Desert, only now the Jerries had them mounted on a tank chassis and unless you caught one by surprise, you didn't stand a chance if you met one.

Early July, we went for a rest and we billeted ourselves in the abandoned houses. Here we were able to have a decent meal. The houses had recently been abandoned and in a hurry. In my billet we found chickens, which we ate and in one garden there were some small piglets running around; the revolver ammo we used to kill these would have wiped out a Jerry battalion! As I had experience of field cooking, I undertook to do the cooking for my crew and with plenty of coal in the cellar and a good cooking stove I was able to turn out an excellent three-course meal – or so it was said by the crew, who much appreciated it and who did the washing up.

We were now in the Calvados country of Normandy. My co-driver found a place where they made the stuff, so he acquired a five gallon jerrycan and returned to us with five gallons of the very best Calvados money could buy. That stuff certainly had a kick in it but, no thank you, not for me. Of an evening he would sit and quaff quite a considerable amount, and on one particular occasion he was warned by Captain Wardlaw to go easy or else he would be forbidden to have any on the tank, so it lasted longer than he originally expected. This area was where Camembert was made; now this I like, so we were able to stock up with adequate supplies. However, it was midsummer and Camembert doesn't take kindly to hot weather so, unfortunately, we had to abandon some before it overcame us.

Then came the attack on Caen, a place it was hoped would fall on D-Day, but it proved a much harder task than was expected. The Regiment moved up early in the morning and I saw tanks the likes of which I had not seen since the days of the tank battles in the Desert. There were thousands of them and it was obvious that we had full intentions of taking it this day. My day, however, was cut short very early on entering a path through a mine field, my tank hit one and blew off my nearside track, so there we stayed and watched from afar the goings on at Caen. When our recovery unit turned up to get us back on the road they were hampered by at least two snipers who were hidden in the woods some 300 yards away. I looked for them from the safety of my turret but I could not pinpoint them, so after one burst of firing, I was able to approximate their position and fired several HE rounds, set on delay, causing air bursts, as well as a couple of bursts of small arms. After that display of strength we didn't hear anything more from the snipers and our fitters were able to get us roadworthy just as the battle of Caen was won, so we joined a rejoicing regiment.

We again moved forward with the Infantry for an assault on the village of La Bijude. Here we met much opposition. All day I was put on to targets and shot them up, then there was a lull and everything quietened down. I dozed at my gun for a few minutes then, bang, we were hit by something. I shot right out of the turret, squeezing past the Tank Commander, and I woke up on the ground wondering what was happening. Shots were coming over so I got behind the tank, then my driver started up and began to reverse, nearly knocking me over. I soon remounted and began firing at targets, mostly foot soldiers running along behind hedges. I had a spot where there was a gap in the hedge and from my position I reckon I scored many hits. I could not get a sight of the gun that had spoilt my slumber because we moved out of his sight and he didn't fire at us anymore. A hairy and lively day but we pulled into Harbour that night with a few marks on the tank but no serious damage, although our ration bin on the outside of the tank had been peppered and we lost some of our rations.

These days of moving up in support of the Infantry were becoming routine, sometimes it was easy going but others not so. Then, early in August, the Squadron moved out to a Village near Falaise. It was at Falaise that we hoped to trap a huge German Army, so in trying to bottle them up we really ran into trouble. We were trying to stop a Jerry column escaping to the North-East and I was doing a lot of shooting. Here, I would like to try and explain the difference between shot (anti-tank) and shell (high explosive).

A shell is a projectile that, when fired, has a pretty high trajectory so if you are on the receiving end you can often hear it coming; it explodes on contact. A shot is fired with a trajectory that is very flat, its velocity is much faster and if you are on the receiving end you hear nothing if it hits the target; if it misses you hear a sharp 'whoosh' as it passes by. It does not explode on contact but if it hits and penetrates the armour, it causes havoc inside the tank.

On this particular day we were watching and shooting up the Jerries. My Tank Commander was standing behind me with his head out of the turret, giving me targets at which to shoot, when 'whoosh' a shot whizzed past and Captain Wardlaw ducked down. I turned to him and said 'You should get your head down before you get it knocked off.' He smiled, then directed me to the flash of the gun. I could see nothing, at first, but then I saw the gun flash again. Before I could take any action the shot struck us, right on the turret ring. Captain Wardlaw came down into the turret and his head rested on my left shoulder. When I glanced round to say something, I saw that he was dead and the contents of his head was oozing out over my jacket. I pushed him gently onto the floor. I then looked under the gun to Sergeant Wright. He was a ghastly white, and was peppered with tiny fragments of shrapnel. Our wireless was smashed, so I shouted through to the driver, 'Yorkie, are you alright?' to which he replied 'Yes'. I told him of the situation in the turret and said to start up and reverse as soon as he could. Just as we got under way another shot came over; it fell right where we had been a moment before. I put my head out of the turret to get a better view of what was behind us as the shots were now falling shorter and shorter.

We were crossing an open field (in reverse) and were approaching a hedge with a pretty deep ditch in front. If we had horses we could have jumped the obstacle with ease but a tank was a different matter. I shouted down to the driver and told him of the obstacle we were about to take. I said 'When I tell you, give it all the revs you've got and for God's sake don't stall, or we're dead ducks.' He revved like hell when he was told and we carved our way through the hedge. When we were out of sight of the gun I told the driver to stop and we then took stock of our position. Sergeant Wright had pulled himself together, so it was decided to return to Squadron HQ. There was nothing we could do for Captain Wardlaw; he had died instantly.

On arrival at HQ the Squadron leader told us to get Captain Wardlaw over to the medical post, then clean up the tank. I was issued with a clean battledress and when all was clean the Signals came to repair our wireless set. We took the rest of the day restocking ammo, petrol, and checking any exterior damage.

Our new Tank Commander was Lieutenant, shortly to become Captain, Akers-Douglas, who had just returned to the Squadron after being slightly wounded. The next day we were at it again. Then we moved to the village of Cazelle where we stayed for nearly a week. Here we were billeted in abandoned houses. I was in a house next to a field in which were several cows. These cows had not been milked for several days it didn't take the lads long to learn how to milk them. We were continually being shelled and one shell landed in the field killing a cow; the half-track was called up, the dead cow hauled into a barn, hung up and the Squadron butcher called in to do his stuff. We lived on fresh beef for some time and fresh vegetables from the gardens around us, our issued tinned rations being stored for emergencies.

After our rest we took part in the encircling of the Germans at Falaise and at times we had some good shooting. The Jerries were really getting cut to pieces, but we weren't overlooked by them; we were shelled mercilessly on several occasions and the multiple mortars were much in evidence. They made a weird noise so they were nicknamed 'Moaning Minnies'. We spent days dashing about trying to close holes where the Jerries were escaping from the trap. The carnage was fantastic. Apart from the damage done to the Jerries, cattle were being slaughtered and left to blow up into grotesque shapes; the stench was nauseating. Dead soldiers were lying around everywhere. A nightmare of a battlefield was all around us. Everybody joined in this chance to finish off the enemy. The Yanks and the Canadians were putting in their pennyworth. Should we be able to seal off this German army and liquidate it, it would certainly shorten the war, but the Germans, who were never stupid when it came to warfare, managed to get some of their troops out, albeit with very heavy losses both in men and material.

The next big battle I was involved with was the fight for the high feature known as Mont Pincon, where we suffered many casualties in the approach, as every move we made was overlooked by the Germans on the high ground and their gunnery was pretty accurate. I had some shots at a MK IV and scored some direct hits; the last I saw it was burning furiously. Then I was directed onto another, but he saw us first and fired. Fortunately, we must have presented an angled target to him, because although his shot hit us it deflected off our turret with a hell of a clang, which shook us all up. My first shot was a hit in the track region, then one or two more of our tanks joined in and Jerry 'brewed up'.

When we got rid of our headaches we set forth again, this time engaging German Infantry who went to ground, so our Infantry went in and dealt successfully with them. When we did eventually attain the summit, things became much quieter. There were mopping up operations going on all around us and when it got dark our Infantry gathered in strength, allowing us to draw back in to Harbour for the night.

This sort of fighting was continuous through the Bocage country, out of the bridgehead and on the Belgium and the Seine. As we travelled eastwards so we saw the evidence of the havoc wrought by the RAF and the American Air Force. The roads were littered with burnt out tanks, lorries, staff cars and a variety of different vehicles, testimony to the accuracy of the bombers.

The weather was appalling, which added to our problems, but 'push on!' was the order of the day and push on we did, meeting sporadic opposition, which was dealt with one way or another.

TANK CREWS FROM MY REGIMENT IN FRANCE AFTER D-DAY.

OUR TANK DECORATED WITH YOUNG LADIES FOLLOWING THE LIBERATION OF BRUSSELS.

CHAPTER 21

Brussels, Arnhem & Wesel

September saw us in Belgium and the advance was speeding up so much that our supporting aircraft never knew where we were and on one occasion gave us a thorough going over with their machine guns. Having sampled this free dose of their medicine, I felt almost sorry for the Germans who were taking it in big doses.

We pushed on to the Somme then on to Brussels where we received a real hero's welcome. Flowers, wine, fruit and kisses were given liberally, but those of us stuck in the turret didn't get very much. I was, however, permitted to stick my head out of the turret for a while and seeing the jubilation brought tears to my eyes. I felt like someone who had done something right for a change and was being shown appreciation in the only way they knew how. This was certainly reward for all that had gone before.

On leaving Brussels we ran into some trouble in the form of a battery of anti-tank guns and by some swift action we managed to deal with eight guns, six of which were captured intact.

On 9th September our Squadron was turned back to assist the Echelons who had been attacked in force and much damage was done to our supplies in the blowing up of thirty odd lorries. Order was quickly restored, mainly by the actions of the cooks and drivers and clerks, who put up a magnificent fight. When the tanks appeared on the scene the attackers fled but they were given a further bloody nose on their way out.

The battle of Arnhem has been written about by many a better man than I. The rights and wrongs of the plan will be talked about for a long time. Far be it from me to make any opinion – all I can tell is how I saw what happened.

The Regiment was sitting on the Escaut Canal when we were briefed on the operation about to take place. The gist of the briefing as I understood was that thirty Corps under General Horrocks were to make a dash up to the North of Holland, from where they would strike at Germany from the North West and push on into the heart of Germany, thus shortening the war. That was the intention…

Airborne drops would be made near the three main bridges at Eindhoven, Nijmegen and Arnhem and 30 Corps would push on to link up with the Airborne troops until they reached Arnhem. The whole operation was to take about ten days.

Well, that sounds very simple and uncomplicated, but there is always the unknown and it was the unknown, or untold, that defeated us.

On 17th September 1944 we witnessed the huge air Armada heading in a northwesterly direction. These, we gathered, were the Yanks. We stayed put until the 20th, when we crossed the Escaut Canal, then early the next day we made the Eindhoven bridge. We were following the Guards

Armoured Division; then on the 23rd, very early, we made for the Nijmegen bridge which we crossed and held for the rest of the day. I slept underneath it that night. There were still some dead bodies on the bridge.

We started to push on to Arnhem, but the terrain over which we were heading was never meant for attacking tanks. The area was as flat as a pancake; only one road with dykes on either side and so the tanks had to run the gauntlet. The weather turned sour on us and it rained like hell. We made a dash up the road but we soon found out that the Jerries had their anti-tank guns well-sited and well-hidden. Then we were told that the bridge at Arnhem was still in enemy hands. At night we were cut off from the Regiment. We reached the river at Driel and stayed there to give what assistance we could to the paras, who were now evacuating the town. We found cover in a barn where we brewed tea. The ceiling of this barn was about seven feet from the ground and above this ceiling was stacked hay. Whilst making the tea my primus cooker flared up for one second, but that was enough to catch the hay. As soon as it was noticed that the barn was on fire we got out in a hurry because we knew that the Jerries would shell us when they realised we were there and, sure enough, the shells started falling thick and fast.

We moved up to the river and here we were given targets at which to shoot. Whilst here, we stood to at last light and at first light in the morning.

On the 26th September, the Airborne troops who could get out were coming over by any means they could. At about 6am, whilst I was making tea, a group of paras came past, wet, tired, clothed in blankets and well and truly fed up. Their remarks to us were unrepeatable; this I understood, but when I offered them a mug of hot tea laced with rum, I was truly surprised when they told me what to do with it. Of course, the paras blamed us for not relieving them at Arnhem and they thought their plight was caused entirely by us who didn't carry out our part of the plan. Obviously, they didn't appreciate the situation on our side of the river, nor did they know of the German strength just North of them, which was a telling factor in their setbacks.

We had been cut off for the second night and were anticipating that we would soon be on German rations of black bread (as POWs), but fortunately the corridor to the Island was re-opened. The Germans seemed to be all round us, but on the 27th we were withdrawn because of the enemy anti-tank guns. Two of our tanks got bogged down and had to wait until nightfall before recovery could be effected.

So ended our part in the Battle of Arnhem…

We were now entering the Winter so we prepared for the cold. The people of Holland were very friendly and put us up in their homes. One family I was billeted with soon realised that we were friendly and not the barbarians the Germans had led them to believe. The man of the house took me out in the garden and from the compost heap withdrew a canvas bag in which he had hidden his silver and valuable items which, he said, he hid from the Germans two years before. Then he went to the small barn and from under the concrete slab he brought out his wireless set which under German rule was strictly forbidden. He took these items indoors and set up the wireless (which worked) and tuned in to the BBC. The mother wept with joy and the son and daughter cuddled me with delight. At dinner they made me some waffles (I provided the flour and sugar) and they had tea and coffee (not ersatz) for the first time in nearly two years. This was typical of all the Dutch families on whom we were billeted.

As the snow fell we camouflaged our tanks white and wore white tank suits. Whilst on the move, nothing we did could keep us warm. Whilst the engine was turning the air was drawn into the turrets by the engine fans, so making any move uncomfortable. For the next few months we were moving about Holland, going to any hot spot where we were needed. Conditions were very bad. The weather was wet and very cold, which made driving most difficult. The roads were choked with slow moving traffic, building up for a push into Germany. I felt the Germans were keeping a special eye on us because everywhere we went we were shelled or mortared. Sometimes on long marches we were lifted onto tank transporters.

November 18th. We joined the Americans in an attack on German soil. We thought that the resistance here was going to be tougher than in the past, but after much hard slogging we eased into Germany and took several villages. The weather was very cold and unpleasant. Whilst we were in the village of Tripsrath inside the German border, we built a two-seater lavatory. When I went to use it in the morning I had to brush away the snow and break the ice – not very comfortable. The fighting for these German villages continued throughout November, but at the end we were solidly entrenched. Monty paid us a visit at the end of

November, then in early December we moved back into Holland where we stayed for three weeks. It was here that our Signal Sergeant, who had replaced Sergeant Wright, realised that I was just as good a radio operator as I was a gunner, so he got me on the wireless watch roll; so for the remainder of the war I was doing as much wireless work as I was doing gunnery. From here, I went on a four-day leave to Louvain in Belgium. I enjoyed a good bath, visited a few bars and saw Rowitch and Landaur performing their duet on the piano.

On my return the news that the Germans were making a last effort attack in the Ardennes put the Regiment on the alert. Rumours were rife that the Boche may drop parachutists in our area, so Christmas was spent on stand to, at dusk and dawn. On New Year's Day, we were out on a recce and whilst we were brewing up tea we were surprised by about a dozen German Messerschmits. They machine gunned us something awful for about half an hour. Up until then the low clouds which had persisted for weeks had grounded all aircraft, so we were taken completely by surprise by the attack. My tank sustained many hits but no damage, neither were there any casualties as we were getting very adept at putting the tank between us and the attacking aircraft. After this attack it was thought that this was a prelude to a German ground attack, so everyone was alerted, but nothing came of the expected attack.

The next episode was when we were bombed by buzz bombs. Two fell near our cooks' lorry, wounding our two cooks, fortunately not seriously. We then started operations to clear the Jerries from the area of the River Ruhr. As we expected the Germans were defending their homeland with much vigour, so we had a hard time making just a few yards progress. The weather was appalling, causing tanks to bog down leaving them as sitting targets for the Jerry anti-tank guns. Then we came against the most powerful tank yet seen, the dreaded 'Tiger', armed with an 88mm gun, which could outshoot at greater range anything the Allies possessed. 'A' Squadron came across a Tiger's lair and suffered badly, but the Tigers were eventually dealt with. All this action took place in the village of Walderfencht, a village very well defended by Tigers, infantry with bazookas and anti-tank guns. It was hardly surprising therefore that any tank that dared to enter was in for a hot reception, which was just what 'A' Squadron got, losing many tanks.

We suffered almost as badly. On the 19th, we set forth with Infantry and immediately ran into a nest of 88s, which knocked out five tanks including our Squadron leader's. He managed to escape injury but his driver, my mate Stan Read, was killed and our Signal Sergeant, Sergeant Bradley, was also killed. This battle raged all day. We suffered many losses, but slowly and surely we were accounting for the anti-tank guns. I was very lucky. Tanks were brewing up all around me but I was somewhat hidden and had a pretty good field of fire from where I could blast the enemy. By nightfall I had fired nearly every round I had in my tank. At this stage the Squadron leader, Major Sir Delaval-Cotter, took over my tank and I was his gunner. At the various stops we made, I was acting as his operator until someone senior could take over. I was working round the clock, doing my gunnery when needed, then at night I was doing the duty of Signal Sergeant, collecting replenishment requirements from the troops, sorting them out, then sending them to RHQ. This was an easy task when we were near RHQ but at times we were some considerable distance away then radio contact became very difficult, as all the frequencies were pretty well jammed. Unless you have heard the din on a battlefield radio network, you can never imagine the noise. You hear other different regiments speaking in plain language, then other different units using Morse – altogether a cacophony of sounds, almost unbeliev-able. This is what I was trying to penetrate to get our requirements through before morning. Sometimes it took all night to get the list through. My knowledge of the Morse Code came in very handy as Morse had a greater range than speech. These were hectic days for me but I was happy to do my part.

On the 26th, we were pulled out of the line for rest and maintenance. Here I contacted the Regimental Signal Sergeant, who was just as keen to see me because it was to him I was sending my messages in Morse. He told me off because I was using an out-of-date code, but this I told him I realised and I didn't know the new codes as I was not carrying out the job as operator, but as I knew he was at the other end and I knew he would know the old codes so long as he got my Squadron code signal, he would read what followed, which was the case.

Whilst we were resting, reinforcements came up and a Squadron Signal Sergeant was appointed, which left me free to concentrate on gunnery, although I was still called upon to do wireless watches. Signs were that we were preparing for a big push into Germany. We were moved back to Nijmegen and attached to the Canadians. The town was full to overflowing with troops. Billets were hard to come by. My crew were eventually put up in a cafe where we had a good rest. I watched an ENSA Concert and saw a couple of films. Then we started loading up our tanks with extra HE ammo. Shells were stacked everywhere possible so long as they didn't interfere with the traverse.

On 8th February 1945, we started an offensive with the biggest artillery barrage known. Everything that could fire an HE shell was having a go. I fired some three hundred rounds that day, then we were sent to an objective, a village called Wyler. The approach march was very sticky and tanks were bogged down owing to the conditions of the road and the flooded areas around. Having got to our target area we then had to shoot the Infantry onto the target, so we had another long shoot at the village. As we penetrated deeper and deeper into Germany, so the resistance became fiercer, even fanatical. We edged forward slowly, but relentlessly, overcoming unbelievable opposition. The ground conditions didn't help and the vast numbers of vehicles using the same roads as we were, slowed up movement. The enemy shelling was proving very accurate and persistent. What with the conditions of the roads which were now being pitted with shell holes, travelling inside a tank was no cruise.

Goch was the next thorn to be picked out, and the defenders weren't going to give up their town without very determined resistance. My personal impression of this attack was as the column in which I was travelling headed for the town, the leading tank was knocked out by one defender with a bazooka. The column was halted and the Infantry were sent in to deal with the offender, but a Spandau machine gun was covering him and as soon as the P.B.I. (Poor Bloody Infantry) showed their faces, he opened up on them. They went to ground. A Spandau is a German machine gun with a rate of fire far greater in excess of anything I have ever heard, so one has to have sympathy for anyone on foot facing such a weapon. At this moment, as far as I could ascertain, two German soldiers were holding up the column and the Artillery were called upon to get rid of these two chaps.

Eventually, the knocked out tank was moved off the road and after the gunners had done their stuff the column, which I was now leading, moved on. The battle raged on. I was given some good targets which included a possible 88mm gun seen half hidden behind a house. The Jocks (our Infantry) made short work of the Jerries and it wasn't long before Goch fell into our hands.

After Goch, the fighting continued and we were being slowed by 88mm SP (self-propelled) guns which seemed to be everywhere. In the second week in March we had a real ding-dong battle and progress was slow and casualties were high amongst the P.B.I. Then we reached the Rhine and I went on leave to England whilst the rest of the Army prepared for the crossing.

I returned to the fray just in time to attend a Regimental Parade complete with Regimental Band, through Goch.

On the 22nd March, we moved to our crossing area at Wessel. The crossing of the Rhine was to be a big event. A very heavy barrage was laid down in which we took part, then the paratroops were dropped to hold a bridgehead for the waterborne troops that were coming behind. We crossed very early on the morning of 25th March and pushed gently forward taking many prisoners. Some of these prisoners were young kids no more than 14 or 15 years old, full of fight but pathetic little boy soldiers; others were pensioners who had done their share in the 1914-18 War.

I was beginning to feel that the fight had gone out of a large number of Germans, as they appeared to be giving up in ever increasing numbers, but we were now moving on to the industrial heart of Germany...

On 6th April, we fought our way into Lingen, where I was to rejoin the 8th Hussars later, then we crossed the Ems, making our way to Bremen. Now the pace was beginning to speed up and enemy resistance was beginning to flag; I think by now they realised that all was lost. However, there were still some German fanatics who didn't want to give in, and we were involved with some of them when, on 7th May, the German High Command surrendered unconditionally to Monty at Luneburg.

THE GENERAL AND HIS BATMAN.

THE AUTHOR AND FRIENDS IN HANOVER – NOTE THE 'SHOP' WINDOW

CHAPTER 22

The General's batman

What were my feelings after five years active service? No more fighting, no more blackouts, no more wondering what tomorrow would bring or who would still be with us. On the night that the ceasefire was signed, I just sat in my turret, alone with my own thoughts. I was not one of those lucky millions in London, New York or Paris who could go out and join the milling crowds and really celebrate. For me, relief was first and foremost – I no longer had to get up in the morning and set out to kill someone (and risk being killed myself).

I was on wireless watch that night. On the following day we moved east of Bremen to accept the surrender of a German Corps. We then moved through another part of Germany, just to show the natives what we looked like. We met with hostile people everywhere. The German civilian population didn't want to acknowledge us as the victors over their invincible nation, or at least this was the feeling I got as I walked around in the different towns. I wasn't impressed with the Germans, who had caused all the misery and suffering throughout the past five years. After this business of damping down the fires, we moved from the Bremen area to Hanover.

Our duties then were guarding certain installations, keeping a tight rein on the thousands of DPs (Displaced Persons) who had been in prison for years and were now roaming loose, looting, raping and stealing anything they could lay their hands on. The German population was terrified of them, and under their present circumstances, there was nothing they could do about them. That's why we had to control them. Then there was the curfew patrol strictly adhered to. This was a job I liked. Our duties on curfew patrol would entail going about the town (smartly turned out) in pairs, and see to it that no one was out on the street after 6pm unless they were in possession of a pass signed by the British Military Control. I would walk through the town and receive catcalls and remarks from the upstairs windows and balconies. The whole population would be watching, and if by chance you caught someone breaking the curfew, no questions were asked (mainly because no one on our side spoke German) they were taken to our base where someone spoke the language. I was determined to learn the language because although I didn't know what they were shouting, I didn't like it because I knew it wouldn't be complimentary. Soon they began to get clever and dodge from door to door and every door was open until we reached it. I took quite a few curfew breakers in and soon the populace were calling me *Das Kleine Fuhrer* – 'the Little Hitler'.

The DPs were proving a bloody nuisance. They were brewing their own hock, getting drunk and then going out on the rampage. 'C' Squadron were then sent to the Herrenhauser area of Hanover. Here we were billeted in flats. I was in a ground floor flat. The regiment were allocated a number of horses, so a riding school was set up. Then we opened the Herrenhausen Opera House. I started to sell coffee on the black market like everyone else. The Germans, whose national drink was coffee, hadn't seen real coffee for years, so we were able to get nearly anything for the real stuff. The price of a pound of coffee was 50 marks, but the Deutschmark was worthless. In fact I had a bundle of 50 million mark notes, worth nothing. An occupation currency was brought in, now this we could use. I went on leave to England and whilst there I arranged with my brother to send me as much coffee he could afford, which he did. Then I started to buy up coffee from all of the other chaps at better prices than they were getting from the Jerries. Hence I cornered the market, so I upped it to the customers. Then I increased my purchase price, which the chaps were all for, and I upped the selling price again, this went on until I was getting 150 marks per lb. As well as two first class cameras, a Telefunken radio, I could obtain nearly anything I required.

One Saturday I went to watch the Wanderers play the regiment at football in the Hanover Stadium; when I came back there was a queue of some twenty people waiting for coffee.

I was doing a bit of riding at this time, bringing back old memories and old skills. When the Hanover Racecourse was opened, I was hoping to do some riding there, as my weight was still only about 8st 8oz. However, the first to open was the Hanomag Stadium for M/C races. There was plenty to do now that all the amenities were gradually coming alive, but the order was still 'no fraternising with the German girls'. However, one would only have to go into the park when the grass was long and shout 'Cops!' to see that this rule was being well-and-truly disobeyed! After all... this was peacetime.

It wasn't long before we were moved and the Squadrons were split up. 'C' Squadron went to Bad Fratzburg in the Hartz mountains. This move came in October, so we knew we were in for a cold winter, but now we had the wherewithal to get warm – warm billets, hot water and a good canteen called the 'Do Drop Inn' I was given a jeep which had been modified with an aluminium cover. In this I would take officers down to RHQ at Woltingrode. This journey was quite easy before the snow came but once the snow came the trip became a nightmare. Christmas came and the celebrations were on a grand scale. By now the fraternisation ban was relaxed and the female population was invited to our dances. I had by now quite a good knowledge of the language, enough to be understood and to carry on a limited conversation.

Spring of '46 came with lots of changes. Men were being demobbed, and our old warhorses, the Shermans, were replaced by armoured cars. Then in April, the Regiment moved all the Squadron into modern barracks at Wolfen-buttel. These barracks had everything; sports grounds, a swimming pool and a first class gymnasium. Naturally, sport was now the thing.

It was here that I said farewell to the 13/18 Royal Hussars (QMO); a regiment I had been very proud to serve in. As long as I live, I shall have many fine memories of comradeship in war and in peace, from my time in England whilst training, when I had some wonderful times with my mates, to being in the thick of the action, when one saw just how soldiering should be done. 'Lilywhites' I shall never forget you!

Before I left, the Regiment restarted the quarter guards, and the best turned out soldier on that guard was excused the guard duty, carried out the duty of 'Stick Orderly' and any soldier who obtained 3 sticks was presented with an arm badge normally worn by the full ranks. Well, as soon as the war finished, I started to 'bull' my boots, so when they restarted the quarter guards, I would always get the stick, in fact I qualified for two. Then the Regiment paraded before the Div. Commander, Major General R.A. Hull who was himself an ex 9th Lancer. My boots attracted his attention; they were really good. After the parade, my Squadron Leader sent for me and told me that I should be before the C.O. in the morning. This really got me worried, because no reason was given and I couldn't think what I had done. However, came the morrow, with best kit and best boots I was marched before the C.O. He congratulated me on my turn out for the parade the day before, then he asked 'How would you like to be the GOC's batman? He has especially asked for an ex-cavalryman.'

Well I wasn't too keen to leave the Regiment, but as I didn't see much promotion coming my way, although I had given my best both in both war and in peace, I decided to take it. This was to be the first staff job I had had in 12 years service. I packed my kit and went to Brunswick to serve the General. His batman was due for demob, so I went to take over. For a week I looked and learnt. At this stage the General was living in one of the two messes 'A' and 'B', but his plans were to turn 'A' mess into his residence. When he interviewed me, he asked if I was married, when I told him I was, he gave me a choice of having a married quarter in the barrack area or a flat in the attic of 'A' mess. I chose the latter, so he had a flat built for me. Prior to this my bunk was down in the basement. One reason why he asked for a cavalryman was because he had some horses, and apart from cleaning his kit, I was to exercise his horses, which I was quite capable of doing. Well I had taken notice of his kit, and I made special note of his boots (my speciality), which I noted were dubbin'd as was required during war. I decided I was now going to polish them, so instead of putting dubbing on them, I put boot polish on them, but I didn't polish them giving the same appearance as dubbin. After weeks of this treatment I asked the General if it wasn't time his riding boots and the normal boots should be polished. He agreed, so I went flat out getting a polish on them.

As GOC he spent lots of time inspecting different regiments and I was determined that on all these occasions he would be the best turned out man on parade. It didn't take long before I achieved this. His boots were like glass. On one occasion when he visited my old regiment 13/18th Hussars, I went along with him to visit my mates. After the parade the C.O. called me over and congratulated me on the General's turnout. This made me feel really good. The General also told me that he felt really well turned out, and that he hadn't seen boots to match his. When the Officers moved out of 'A' mess, I was put in charge of his residence as Major-domo. I sent to England for my Blue No. 1 dress (8th Hussars) which I wore on dinner nights, all very smart. The General then sent for his wife and arranged for my wife to join me.

We had a German cook, and as I could now speak German pretty well, we got on very well. I liked this job very much and I know that what I achieved was much appreciated. When the General went on leave to England, he took me with him, by plane and when he visited Denmark, I went too.

One of the General's perks was a shooting lodge and fishing rivers in the Hertz mountains, where he would go at every possible opportunity. He would invite the senior officers of the Division for a shoot which was always a busy time for me, but, we had our time off in the evening, when the driver and I would get out the rubber dinghy and go spinning on the lake. The General gave me a fishing rod and flies and showed me how to cast, and where, then he would go off, leaving us to do the best we could. On one occasion when he came in for lunch with about a dozen large trout, he asked to see my catch. I had nothing to show him, so he took my rod, looked at the fly and knot it was tied with, passed that okay, then he asked me to give him a demonstration cast, this was satisfactory, then he took my line, cast into the river and lo and behold a good sized trout attached itself to the line. 'There,' he said, 'it's easy isn't it.' The whole time I was with him I never caught one trout!

Then back in Brunswick one evening, he went with his G1, G2 and his ADC on a duck shoot. When we arrived he gave me a shotgun and a haversack full of ammo. He then put me in position, told me where the other guns would be so I wouldn't shoot them, then we waited. As dusk fell one or two birds came in, then they came in their droves and the shooting started. The birds came in so low I could have hit them with my rifle butt. However, I blasted away for about 15 minutes, then everything quietened down. The General called to bring in the birds. They all had dozens, me – zero. The General asked for the remainder of my ammo.

'I've fired them all, sir.'

Silence. 'And you didn't get one?' he said.

I hung my head and slunk away. So ended my first duck shoot. Anyway, what would I have done with a dead duck when the General was supplying me with all my food, including roast duck. I never did improve. Give me a rifle any day!

The General's wife joined him and she took over the running of the household, which took a certain amount of chores off my plate. I was able to give the horses more attention. My wife arrived and the General told me I could use his Mercedes staff car to collect her at Brunswick airport. This indeed was a pleasure for both me and my wife. The flat that the General had made for me was very comfortable. It was complete with bathroom, central heating and a sitting room – all fully furnished. In view of the size of the attic, we also had enough room to have a table tennis table, where my wife and I used to play quite often. We invited any of the staff who wanted to play to come up.

When the General went on a three week holiday to the Hertz mountains, my wife and I went along and we were put up at the OR's hotel, all expenses paid. Here we learnt to play Badminton, although I had learnt in Egypt. My wife and I won the Doubles and Singles title for guests in our third week. We didn't do any skiing but we used to go for walks up the mountain and we tried our hands at sledding. We had a wonderful time.

The General then went to Camberley for a conference and I accompanied him. I saw him into Camberley then he sent me on a week's leave with instruction to join him at his house in Thame. When we returned to Germany he told me that he had been appointed Commandant to the Staff College. Some time later he gave me the choice of staying as batman to the new General or returning to my Regiment. He paid me the compliment of saying he would very much like to take me with him to Camberley, but serving soldiers were not allowed as batmen. I asked him if I could go back to my first Regiment, the 8th Hussars. He then arranged for my wife and I to go together to Lingen where the 8th were stationed. A married Quarter was waiting for me. He said he was very sorry to lose me but even as Commandant he couldn't break regulations, so I went to Lingen to the 8th Hussars.

MEMBERS OF THE REGIMENTAL BAND.

CHAPTER 23

A Hussar again

In the summer of 1946 I returned to my Regiment, with whom I had served throughout the Desert Campaign. I found many a familiar face, all of whom welcomed me back into the fold. I was placed in Major Firth's Squadron and almost immediately he promoted me to full Corporal. I was once again delegated to the Gunnery wing as an Instructor. Like every unit in the Army, my Regiment were suffering from a shortage of manpower. So many men were being demobbed and not enough replacements were coming in.

My hobby these days was photography. I had acquired a first class camera and learnt to use it with good effect; in fact, I became acquainted with a professional photographer, he was German and lived in Lingen. He gave me a good book on the subject and through him I learnt to develop and print and enlarge my own negatives. With his help I acquired the equipment to carry on this hobby. His name was Heinz Schelm. I started taking photos of subjects of interest within the Regiment such as; I took some very good snaps of the Regimental Beagles; our RSM, Tom Hegarty, was an excellent horseman and he had acquired a bay gelding which proved to be a good jumper, so he trained it up and entered it for the Olympia Horse Show and I took some excellent pictures of him over the jumps. This year I had five of my pictures accepted for the Regimental Journal. Major Phillips, our 2nd I.C. was also a keen photographer so we often had chats about cameras, lenses and accoutrements. Incidentally, RSM Tom Hegarty did very well at Olympia. At Christmas the Regiment entertained all the children of Lingen which probably helped to dispel any bad ideas they held about the English, all part of the re-education plan.

Sport played a big part in the life of the troops in Germany and with my past achievements and knowledge I was soon involved. I was sent to the PT School at Belefelt on a football referee's course (passing with 99%) and a short hockey umpire's course (which was not tested).

I assisted 'B' Squadron to win the Squadron Tug-o-War by coaching them. Our jockeys and show jumpers were doing well all over Germany and late spring and early summer were spent in training new recruits (National Servicemen). The weather was getting hotter, so training was outside. In the early summer, 'B' Squadron went on a visit to the Mohnsee of 'Dam-Busters' fame. We stayed a week under canvas and here the youngsters learnt something of living rough, cooking whatever they could come up with. Some ate well; others didn't, but by the end of the week those who were starving had learnt something. 'A' Squadron rejoined us from the U.K. (Warminster School of Infantry) where they had been for nine months as a demonstration squadron. From all accounts they did a marvellous job there. The manpower situation was becoming critical so it was that one squadron ('C') was put into suspended animation. The two remaining Sabre squadrons taking it upon themselves to carry out the training of individuals, then troop and squadron training.

In the Autumn, the War Office saw fit to make every man in the Army pass a physical fitness test. This proved very hard for some of us 'old 'uns' but the '10 mile bash' didn't defeat me. This was a run/walk of 10 miles, at the end of which we were required to shoot five rounds at a target at 200 yards range– all to be completed in a set time and in full marching order, carrying a rifle. I will admit that after completing this task I was dead beat and stiff for days!

On the 4th October, I was promoted to Sgt. and entered the Sergeants Mess. The R.S.M., Tom Hegarty welcomed me into the Mess. I felt really thrilled that I was now a member of the most exclusive club in the world. My own thoughts were that at last I've made it, and my work has at last been appreciated, because work I did. Everything seemed to be going all right. My wife was pregnant and the rumours were that we were going home.

At Christmas the Regiment gave the Germans a huge party for about 700 children, at which I assisted and as my German was pretty good by now, I enjoyed myself almost as much as the children. After Christmas we started packing up ready for the move home to the U.K. It was a very busy time. We had to hand over all our tanks so they had to be brought up to standard, not that they were below standard.

On the 4th February the advance party left. The Regiment were heading for Leicester, to an old R.A.F. Airfield. This was a Nissen hutted camp, pretty dilapidated and certainly not as comfortable as the Barracks we had just left in Germany. My wife left with the main party, but as there were no married quarters allocated to us yet, she had to go to a transit camp in Hull. When I first saw her there, I was disgusted with the conditions under which she was living. Small rooms, like cells, communal baths and toilets which were filthy. Communal dining hall, where the children ran riot and created a din. The table cloths were bed sheets, often stained with cocoa, or tea, and the food was disgusting. As my wife was 6 months pregnant at the time, I felt very concerned, so I had a word with the Camp Commandant. He admitted all the faults, but as he said, he could do nothing about it. He did change our accommodation to a Nissen hut which was one degree better, but still most unsatisfactory.

It wasn't long before the Regiment was split up doing various jobs throughout the Midlands. One job was to guard some W.D. Property against squatters. I was sent up to Yorkshire in charge of 5 trumpeters. Major Lowther was G.I. in Northern Command, and Command Artillery were putting on a tattoo around Yorkshire. Major Lowther sent to the regiment for the trumpeters, so as an ex-trumpeter, I was selected to take this party. Whilst I was at Leeds, I received a telegram that my wife was ill, so I had to get over to Hull in a hurry. I found my wife was about to have a premature birth. She was rushed to Driffield and there gave birth to our son who weighed in at 2½lbs – two months premature. I went back to Leeds to complete the tattoos at Sheffield and Bradford, then back to Leicester. On arrival the C.O. sent for me to congratulate me on our performance and bearing during these tattoos.

The Regiment were soon allotted married quarters in Glen Parva Barracks about 4 miles from the air field. I was one of the fortunate families to be allotted one of these. I soon acquired a motor cycle to make the journey to and from camp. For some unknown reason the C.O. decided to send me on an accounts course at the Pay Corps at Devizes. I enjoyed this course as I liked figures. I came away with 'Distinguished' marks 99%. On my return I was given a job in the P.R.I.'s office. P.R.I. is the President of the Regimental Institute who deals with all the accounts of the Regimental funds, Band funds and is responsible for the welfare of the Regiment, so I had a big job on my hands. It was a job I very much enjoyed, and I did very well. On my weekends I was very active with sport, refereeing some football match, or umpiring a hockey match. I got a regular job umpiring for Loughborough College.

The Regiment's main task was to train Territorial Army Regiments from the Midlands by the running of summer TA camps in East Anglia. The only snag was manpower; the Regiment could only muster 196 men in December 1948, so we could only field two squadrons, one for administration, the other to keep our few tanks on the road and up to scratch for the TA to use at their summer camps.

The Regiment still maintained horses, and where better to hunt than in the midst of Quorn country? Fodder was hard to come by, so like a good cavalry regiment, we grew our own hay around the airfield and stored it in Nissen huts. Unfortunately, nobody told us that hay stored inside should be perfectly dry, otherwise internal combustion will set it alight. That is exaclty what happened, but luckily sufficient feed was salvaged, and a valuable lesson learnt.

Life was very hectic, what with T.A. Camps throughout the summer, and various other chores throughout the winter, life was full. My married quarter was inside Glen Parva Barracks, right next to the gymnasium, so every free evening I had, I would go over and play badminton. Tom Hegarty was a regular opponent and he was an expert, but we used to have some good tournaments. I was getting quite proficient, as well as keeping fit for my role as referee.

At the T.A. camps in Norfolk, my role as PRI Sergeant was mainly to organise entertainment for the troops. We held dances in the village of Swaffham which were always well attended and well appreciated, as there were no amenities at hand other than the canteens and messes. I also arranged with AKC (Army Kinema Corp) to show films. At the same time I was Sergeants Mess Treasurer, so I was kept busy.

Back in Leicester my book-keeping kept me going. Preparing accounts for audit used to keep me up until 4am some mornings, but as long as I had a radio giving me background music, I could work on until the books balanced. The reports of the auditors was sufficient compensation. Of course I was only assisting my officer, Major Sir Edward Malet, Bart., who often kept going long after I had gone home, and it was he who finally produced the accounts. His work as Welfare Officer was very much appreciated, especially among the married personnel. He was the perfect diplomat when he had some very sticky problems to sort out; such as on one occasion, a wife of a Corporal, who thought she should have been allotted a quarter, came to the camp with her 5 children and parked herself on the steps of the C.O.'s office. 'Neddy' sorted it out to everyone's satisfaction.

I had now obtained my 1st Class Referee's Certificate. This enabled me to referee army matches up to the final, so I was getting plenty of matches. In fact as I was the senior referee of the district, I was voted on the civilian roll and also onto the Leicester Committee. One Saturday I was on the line at Filbert Street, the home of Leicester City who that year were in the 1st Division and did very well in the Cup.

My wife, son and I went home to Addlestone for a holiday. Whilst there my Dad got out his Austin 7 from his garage. The car had been laid up since the outbreak of war. This car was in immaculate condition, considering its age of 12 years. It didn't take much starting once he had his battery charged. Then he asked me if I wanted to buy it. I jumped at it and he only asked £30.00. This was my first car. It was small, but very reliable. It got me from Addlestone to Leicester without a hitch, and I was very pleased with it.

This was peacetime once again and soldiering was very good. As far as I could see at this moment throughout the world, nobody was fighting us, so we looked set for a long spell of quiet. 1949 was coming to its end. It had been a very hard year, but in many cases very rewarding. The Regiment had made many friends. The T.A., the locals and anybody who needed their services. The local hunt were entertained to a hunt Ball organised by the Regiment, at which I officiated. This was the poshest ball I had ever seen. It went on until early morning, and as a sober official, I didn't see anybody as sober, when I left at 5.00 a.m. I'm only thankful that I didn't have to clear up the mess.

Again came rumours of a move. The W.D. had decided to form a strategic reserve. This I understood was an Independent Brigade ready and equipped, prepared to go anywhere that their presence was required. This brigade was based at Tidworth, so that is where we were headed. A married man in the army has to be prepared to pack up and move at short notice. So, within a period of two years we were on the move for the second time. Packing up the PRI Office and stores didn't take too long. February 1950 saw us settled in Mooltan Barracks. An old and dilapidated cavalry barracks of the early nineteenth century. Before we moved in, a party moved down to paint the Barracks from top to bottom.

I was given a quarter above the Officers Mess. This was a prestige quarter, and it was near my office. The beagle's kennels were just outside the back door.

This appeared to be the time for a change over in Command. Our CO, Lt Colonel Goulburn left us for higher command. I knew the Colonel for many years, in fact since I joined as a band boy in 1934. He saw the Regiment through thick and thin, and war and peace. Then our RSM Tom Hegarty decided to retire to civvy street. Tom was a rough rider in the cavalry and was one who would break in new horses – he was also a riding instructor. We were all sorry to lose these two stalwart 8th Hussars. Major Phillips took over command of the Regiment. He was recently married and some of us were guard of honour at his society wedding.

Tom Hegarty's replacement was an Irish Guardsman, named Tom Leckie, and although he wasn't an 8th Hussar, it didn't take him long to become one.

CHAPTER 24

Trouble brewing in Korea

The worldwide news at this time was centred on a small unknown country called Korea. I had never heard of the place, although I did very well at geography both at school and since, however, I was to learn quite a lot about it before too long.

Soldiering continued in Tidworth. The stables were in good form, that is the horses that were in them, and the beagles were well exercised, old Paddy Munroe saw to that. They said that Paddy saw service in the Charge of the Light Brigade. I didn't believe that, but he certainly saw lots of service somewhere!

As the year drew on, so the news coming from Korea became more dicey, then, in June, the North Koreans, egged on by the Russians invaded the South. This caused ructions in the United Nations and in America. The Americans promptly sent in troops from Japan to assist the South Koreans, who by then had nearly been pushed into the sea. The Security Council of the United Nations called on all members to send aid to South Korea, so our Government decided to send 2 Brigades. One from nearby Hong Kong, the other was our Brigade at Tidworth. So, panic stations. We were to be equipped with the new 52 ton Centurion tanks, so men were sent to Lulworth for gunnery & Bovington for driving and maintenance. Although we had never seen a Centurion, we were expected to be fully mobile within two or three months. Parties were sent to the factories to hustle the workers. All seemed to be going well, but then they suddenly withdrew our MK II and issued us with MK III.

To think that some six months previously I had thought I had seen the last of war, and now I was going to be up to my eyes in it again! Why did I have to be in such a famous Regiment, with such a good name on the battlefield?

Training was really going flat out, movement orders were issued and packing up was well under way. Reservists were called up, and some of my ex-buddies rejoined us. We were soon brought up to battle strength. The Sergeant's Mess closed three days before the off, so instead of having a farewell party, I first obtained permission to open the bar in the Sergeant's Mess, then I approached our local brewers to supply a complete bar on a sale or return basis. I was going by air, so I was on the rear party-cum-advance party, and I was able to keep the Sergeant's Mess bar open up until the last night. My very good friend, Taffy Morgan, turned up from Netley, where he was serving in some administrative capacity; I had not seen him since he was captured in the desert in 1941. Then on the last night we had a real party when another old 8th Hussar, Jimmy Paviour, turned up. Jimmy was our soccer captain before the war. He was demobbed in 1937 and became Captain of the England Amateur team. The party that night was a real cracker, especially as towards the end I made a punch cum cocktail with all the part bottles that were left. It put the finishing touches to all the stragglers.

The movement orders were: the Regiment would sail from Southampton for Korea on HMT Empire Fowey on October 11th. A rear party remained behind to do the final clearing up, then they would fly out, arriving in Korea some two weeks before the Regiment, acting as the advance party.

The Regiment moved out on schedule. The wives were promised that for the duration of the emergency, they could stay put and not be moved. When the final clearing up had been completed, we moved out early one morning to Lyneham RAF Station, there to catch our plane. Before we had gone too far we noticed an extra lorry had joined our convoy, but nothing was done. We passed through the gates of the RAF Station amid full security, including the extra lorry. When we disembarked from our lorries and made our way to the plane, some shadowy figures followed us, on closer inspection, we saw our wives had come to wish us farewell. How they got in and out again I'll never know.

Our flight out was interesting but uneventful, although in parts a trifle rough. We travelled in uniform because all the stops were RAF bases, until we got to Manila where we were placed in the hands of the USAF, who took us on to Japan. From Tokyo Airport we went by train to the southernmost tip of Japan, to the naval base of Sasebo. We stayed the night with the Americans, then, early the following morning we set sail on the 'Kara Maru' for Pusan, where we were greeted by an American Band playing music in march time. We disembarked and were sent to a dilapidated barracks, which we called Jap Camp. This was to be the 8th Hussars base for some time.

My job as PRI Sergeant was to make contact with the Canteen services, and get in supplies of beer, cigarettes and toilet requisites and anything that might be called comforts. The NAAFI had not reached Korea, nor Japan, so I contacted the Australian Canteen Services. They did us very well, I was able to get almost unlimited supplies of beer and spirits and English cigarettes.

I was soon to learn that the American troops were strictly rationed with alcoholic drinks. It appeared that the League of American Women had this restriction passed through Congress. Whilst we were in Korea we were under Command of the Americans, General MacArthur no less, therefore all of our stores, food and equipment were supplied by them. We had just 2½ weeks to prepare for the Regiment's arrival, so we worked very hard. We drew up sufficient beds and bedding, kitchen equipment for all Squadrons, plus the Officers' Mess. Our QM, Major Charlie Hedley, worked wonders with the Americans. He obtained certain items of equipment that were not on the schedule. The Regiment turned up and were able to move into Jap Camp in comparative comfort, thanks entirely to Charlie.

My impression of Korea was that this country stank. The smell was so permanent that no matter what you did you couldn't lose it. The country was so far behind the rest of civilisation, that it is no wonder it was unheard of. There were no tarmac roads, no sewage, the toilets were just a hole in the wall. Each house had a trench running outside their windows into which went their sewage. In the morning, a native would appear with a scoop on a pole, scoop out the sewage and throw it into the road to lay the dust, hence the permanent smell.

By November, the temperatures were well below zero and much worse to come. In the summer the heat was well into the 100s, the mosquitoes were almost a bigger pest than the 'Gooks' (the troops' name for the Koreans). Special medical precautions had to be taken. We had to parade each night to take salt tablets and palerdrin anti-malaria tablets. After dusk, shirt sleeves had to be rolled down and insect repellent rubbed on the bare skin. The inoculations we had would have punctured a pincushion. The medical authorities reckoned they found mosquitoes in Korea that had never been seen elsewhere.

Getting on with the preparations went smoothly. It was not surprising that alcohol in the form of whisky was better than any currency with which to trade with the Yanks. Through this medium we were able to obtain many extras for the Regiment; for example, we managed to get a generator and have the whole camp wired, including bulbs, for a few bottles of the hard stuff.

One bitter taste, to my mind, was the pay and allowances made to the British troops in Korea. Every nation who sent troops to Korea gave them extra pay in the form of overseas allowance and some paid hardship money. When our Government was approached they sent out a team to investigate the situation. This team came to my PRI Store. One Officer picked up a bar of Lifebuoy Toilet Soap and asked what that bar of soap would cost in England. When I told him 10d. he put it down and asked me the same questions of cigarettes, beer, etc. then he remarked 'It's no dearer here than it is in England, why do you need an overseas allowance?. What could I say to that? So we got nothing until they decided to pay us a bonus when we got home – about £90. The Australian Army had their pay doubled whilst they were serving in Korea and a married man who made an allowance to his wife had it doubled. The bonus certainly did not compensate for the hardships we underwent with the climatic conditions, let alone the horrific fighting we had to do.

CHAPTER 25

A very nasty war

The Regiment docked in Pusan on 14th November. The temperatures were well below zero – 22 degrees of frost was recorded. I went aboard with the rest of the advance party and met an old school pal who was a W.O. in the R.A.O.C. The Regiment had had an uneventful voyage. I went into the bar on board and had a drink with the RSM Tom Leckie. From our description of Korea he wasn't all that keen to leave the comfort of the Empire Fowey. The American band gave them a noisy welcome and on disembarkation they passed under an arch on which was painted 'Through these Portals passed the best God-dam Army in the World!'

The situation on the Korean Peninsular was at that time a bit confusing but let me bring you up to date with the War so far.

In the late summer of '50, the North Koreans crossed the 38th Parallel, therefore invading the South. The Americans had withdrawn from Korea a year before leaving the South to defend themselves. Against the Russian trained and equipped North, the South didn't stand a chance, so the Northerners had it nearly all their own way once they decided to invade. Once the U.N. decided to assist the South, the Americans reacted pretty quickly and although the ROK had advanced almost down to Pusan, the Yanks built up a considerable force in the Pusan box and were able to contain the advance.

The first British contingent of two regiments of the 27 Brigade from Hong Kong landed in Pusan at the end of August. Although they were under strength, they were welcomed by General MacArthur, who needed all the help he could get! The American build up in Pusan was sufficient to enable the General to make a counter-attack by mid-September, which with the help of a sea-borne landing by American Marines at Inchon, was a complete success. Soon the Americans were across the 38th Parallel and heading North. By the 20th October the British 27th were in Pyongyang, the capital of North Korea. By the time the 8th Hussars had landed, and it took some time to gather their tanks together, unless MacArthur was going to invade China, the war looked as though it would be over by Christmas. Then he suffered a setback and in his own words 'A new war is beginning'. The Chinese had invaded Korea and the initial shock to the Americans was disastrous. Almost as soon as they were organised 'A' Squadron were up on flats heading North with 'B' Squadron following hard on their heels. Then the Americans got hit by the Chinese and started retiring. Before 'A' and 'B' Squadrons could get into action they were ordered to return. The Centurion tank was 52 tons and very large. The tracks or roads in Korea were not built for such monsters so many difficulties were experienced in manoeuvring them among the hills and now among the retreating Americans and the refugees that were swarming South. In fact, in a very short time the roads to the South were almost impassable. The whole of 29th Brigade made Pyongyang and were placed in defence of that city. It was obvious to one and all that the fortunes of war had once again changed and the chances of being home by Christmas had gone. The retirement was speeding up until it was a retreat, then the retreat became a panic.

I was in an Echelon approaching Pyongyang to replenish our tanks, the southerly flood was holding us up. I saw men abandoning their vehicles and hitching a lift on others. I watched a large Dodge come to a halt. I saw the driver and his co-driver get out, collect their personal belongings and thumb a lift. I went over to this lorry and after a check over it, I realised the only fault with it was it had run out of petrol. I got a five-gallon jerrycan full of petrol, put it in the Dodge and drove it away. I kept this vehicle as a PR1 Store for the rest of our stay in Korea. When my Squadron Leader saw this lorry he asked me how I had come by it. I explained how I had salvaged it and he said that it must be returned, but by the time we had got back to the River Imjim the regimental vehicle strength had increased by about 30 vehicles, lorries, trucks, jeeps and even half-tracks, so my contribution was overlooked. I had seen several retreats on the Western Desert, but nothing like the one I was witnessing right then. The British Brigade had orders to retire, so they started an orderly withdrawal, but if you could imagine a gold rush in the American West, then that was what I was watching; all heading South as fast as they could go; no order; no orderly columns. The fastest was the first and to hell with the others.

The 29th Brigade met the 27th Brigade coming out. The 27th asked 'What the hell have you been doing?' The 29th replied 'Coming to get you out of trouble.' Also, as the two Squadrons were getting on with the business of stopping the flow of Chinese, an American soldier said to one tank crew, 'You want to get the hell out of here while there is time.' The driver of the tank shouted, 'Get off our bloody pitch!' The Yanks were burning dumps of petrol, clothing and ammunition. The sky was black with smoke, very little of it was put down to enemy action. Both British Brigades withdrew according to plan and acted as rearguard to the Americans. Although they came back they did not encounter an angry Chinaman. In fact, by the time they reached the river the Chinese were some ten days behind. They couldn't keep up with the retreating Americans. The poor tank crews of the 8th Hussars were getting messed around something awful. First they were told to go North, then by the time they got underway they were told to halt, having switched off their engines, they were given fresh orders to retire in support of the Infantry. The temperatures were about 30 degrees of frost. The tanks were covered with ice and the crews had no way of getting warm. I was with the Echelon wandering around trying to locate the tank squadrons who were on the move. We eventually caught up with them at about midnight. I went round with my supplies of goodies and was much appreciated. Now that I had extra transport, I was able to carry more stock so I didn't have to go back to replenish so often, saving petrol. We eventually got back south of the Han River where the retreat stopped and the river formed a line of defence which was to be held.

By December 6th, the Regiment was together for the first time. Higher command decided that the Centurions, which were still on the secret list and too valuable to expose to unnecessary risk, were to remain south of the river. To sum up, the Americans and the U.N. forces that arrived in time had a smashing victory in breaking out of the Pusan box and forcing the enemy back the full length of the Peninsular to the Yalu River. The Chinese then came into the picture. It was first rumoured that some 300,000 had crossed the Yalu but this was modified later. With the arrival of the Chinese, the Americans had panicked and ran back as fast as they could leaving the British 27th and 29th Brigades to fight a rearguard action. Arriving at the Han River in the first week of December. We had lost one tank in the scatter-back but this was not due to enemy action and there was sufficient time to dismantle what could be taken off, and the hulk was blown up, after which it was dealt with by the U.S.A.F. directed by an 8th Hussar Officer.

So we spent Christmas on the Han River. The cold was so intense that the tank engines had to be started every hour, day and night. In the morning straw was placed around the turrets and around the tracks and suspension and set alight to break the grip of frost that occurs when metal touches metal in a very deep frost. The crews had to be very careful not to touch the tank with bare hands because the skin would be torn off if they did. Shaving was most difficult. If you dipped your razor into a mug of boiling water, by the time the razor reached your face it would be frozen. Tea would freeze almost before it reached the mug. Such were the hazards of fighting in this foul country.

I was still dealing with the Australian Canteen Services, but it didn't take long for the N.A.A.F.I. to wake up to the fact that there was money to be made out of the Korean War, so they set up shop in Pusan, which is where I would go for re-stocking. Of course, every transaction was booked and the accounts were kept up to date and accurate, as under normal conditions. One good advantage of being fed by the Americans was that they certainly had the food. The turkeys were huge and the boxes of steaks were something else, the likes of which I had never seen before. I was receiving parcels of comforts for the Regiment from all over the world. The CO's wife, Mrs Phillips, had organised our wives back home into knitting comforts and these, along with the rest, were very much appreciated by the troops. Gloves, Balaclava helmets and socks were gratefully received. All these were distributed to the tank crews first. I received many parcels of books and magazines. These were also much appreciated as in Korea there were no amenities, no shops, cafes or cinemas, so the troops had to rely on their own means of comfort, which didn't extend very far and that's where the books and magazines came in useful.

Rumours were going around that the Regiment was going to be sent out of Korea. Some said home, some said Japan, but before either of these came to fruition the Regiment was engaged in a terrific struggle with the Chinese, which resulted in the loss of many good men. I was not there, but the stories that reached us back in the Echelon were horrific. On New Year's Eve the battle started. By New Year's Day the Chinese were pushing forward. Captain Astley-Cooper, who was in charge of our Recce troop, gathered some Cromwell tanks from 7th RTR and Gunners OP tanks and formed what was to be known as 'Cooper Force'. He was on the North side of the Han. On the night of 2nd – 3rd January the Chinese attacked the Ulsters in force and Cooper Force was involved. The Chinks swarmed in like ants and no matter which way the tank crews looked there were Chinks. Cooper Force was called upon time and again to assist the hard-pressed Infantry, but they were themselves under heavy attack. It was reported that the Chinks were swarming all over the tanks, but by morning the situation was under control. The tanks replenished having fired all their ammo. Plans were laid to move South of the River. Although the Chinese seemed to have gone there were still pockets proving a menace and it was one of these pockets that finally put paid to our very brave Captain. Although the Chinese didn't get what they came for, they did cause us many casualties. The Infantry suffered many casualties, dead, wounded and missing.

Then came an episode that must go down in the annals as the biggest cock-up in history. Through no fault of the 8th Hussars, the Regiment found itself split between Japan and Korea. 'A', 'B' and RHQ reached Kure in Japan when the order to get out of Korea was rescinded, leaving 'C' Squadron on its own in Korea with the tanks of the other Squadrons.

I got to Kure, which was an Australian base in Japan. Here, I liased with our friends, the ACS to set up a canteen. I was allocated a good-sized room so I opened up a canteen to which the troops could come and have a good drink. The troops who were lucky enough to get to Kure enjoyed their relaxation, but all good things come to an end and it wasn't long before we were back in Korea and, once again, up the 'sharp end'. The cold at this time was still our biggest enemy. There was nothing we could do about 100% antifreeze which didn't stop the tanks freezing up, nights were disturbed by the starting up of vehicles every hour. Temperatures were recorded at 40 degrees of frost.

I was sent to Pusan, which was a regimental base, and there I set up a store and office. From here I supplied the forward troops. A Sergeants' Mess was set up and here the Mess Caterer, Paddy Redmond, entertained our American friends. I was building up a stock for the forthcoming Paddy's Day and I was sent for by the O.C. and told to prepare the books, stocks and accounts, to hand over my job of PR1. I was going up the sharp end to take over a troop of tanks, as Troop Sergeant. The handover was completed with nothing untoward reported, then the day before Paddy's Day I went up to the sharp end. Now I hadn't been near a tank since leaving Germany in 1948 and I certainly didn't know anything about the Centurion, so I was going to have to learn fast. I was to take over as Troop Sergeant to 4th Troop 'C' Squadron and, incidentally, I was to take over the terrible twins, these were Troopers Ken Hall and Ken Webster, both good at their jobs but both inclined to be a bit on the rough side. First I was taught about the gun. This came easy as I was used to tank guns, then I learned the intricacies of the turret and its workings with regards to the stabilising. I soon learnt to control fire and tank orders. Eventually I got the confidence of the crew and I was prepared for anything that may come up. I really didn't have much time to celebrate Paddy's Day as I was reading up on the Centurion. I will admit I was very rusty when it came down to it.

On the firing line there was nothing big going on. Orders were that only one tank squadron was to operate at the sharp end at any one time. At this time 'B' Squadron were up supporting the Infantry battalions of the Brigade. They were carrying out probing patrols, and counter attacks on the Chinese attempts to infiltrate our positions. 'C' Squadron took over from 'B' Squadron on the 30th May, so we moved up. I was now a fully-fledged Tank Commander and Troop Sergeant. My crew soon got used to me and we quickly got down to a routine; whenever we stopped the first thing off the tank was our Bivvy, which we put up beside our tank. Wires were strung from the tank carrying electricity and the extended headset, then the brew can was put into action and once we were settled in out came the playing cards and crib board. This we had off to a fine art. We reckoned that the moment the tracks stopped we would be playing cards within ten minutes. We were carrying out exercises with a ROK Company and doing various experiments such as crossing flooded paddy fields, these tests were carried out against various other tanks and the Centurion came out the most efficient. We climbed mountains where even the goats refused to go. There were some nasty traps on the paddy fields. Large six foot square and about six foot deep cesspits filled with sewage, all ready to be spread on the paddy.

On one occasion we pulled up on a paddy field and one of the tanks pulled up alongside one of these pits. The Tank Commander hadn't realised that the pit was there so he leapt off the tank as usual – straight into the pit. Whew! When he got out the crew deserted and weren't to be seen around for some hours. Such are the perils of Korea.

On the various probes we made with the Infantry, testing their strength, we learnt much about the Chinese; they were masters of camouflage. On one occasion I was watching a hill where the Chinks were supposed to be. I looked and with my binoculars scanned every inch of the hill, but saw nothing but trees and bushes, but no other movement. The Infantry edged forward and my gun was loaded to give them support if needed. They hadn't gone very far when the bushes came to life and started shooting up my friends. I went into action with m/g and shell fire. The element of surprise was with the Chinese. This sort of trick was to be used by them to great effect in the near future. There was a steady move forward by the Allies. The object was to straighten the line at the 38th Parallel. Certain gains were made in other places and these were harder to achieve. I thought these moves were preparatory to an all-out offensive. Spring had sprung and the weather was warming up although the rain was proving a nuisance. I went out with a half Squadron and 'B' Squadron under command of our C.O. Lt. Colonel Sir William Lowther. We went out on a recce 'Swan' just to see the strength of the Chinese. We pushed on about 18 miles into enemy territory. I was in the lead for nearly all of the probe. Unfortunately, my driver left the road and threw a track just before we reached the limit of the push. I and my crew, with the aid of the fitters, spent about 2 hours getting back on the road, then we rejoined the group. On the 21st we went on a small recce with a Company of the Northumberland Fusiliers and returned at about 5 p.m. when we connected up with our bivvy, made tea and settled down to the crib board. We played until about 10.30pm, then settled down to sleep.

At about midnight I was awakened by the sound of small arms fire. You might say that this was not surprising as we were in a battle zone. Well, when you have been in as many battle zones as I had, you get to know what is usual and what is not. This was not; especially as the firing was getting heavier and nearer. My crew were by now awake so I told them to get packed up whilst I contacted my Troop Leader, Lt. Hurst. He agreed with me that there was something afoot so the troops were alerted. Permission to brew up was given so long as it was under cover. Lt. Hurst went to see the Acting Squadron Leader, Captain Ormrod. All troop leaders were called for an 'O' Group (short for 'Order Group' where orders are issued), then information came through from Brigade Headquarters that the Chinese had crossed the river in force and were attacking the Gloucesters. We were packed up and ready to move to their support by first light. Came the dawn and the Squadron moved. The four troops were split up to go to the assistance of the Infantry, who had been under attack since midnight. I was sent to assist the NFs and all morning I was directed onto parties of Chinamen trying to outflank the NF over the hills.

Late in the afternoon, the NFs were holding a hill which overlooked a valley. The Chinese were trying to dislodge them, but without success. Then a column of American jeeps turned up from behind me. The Officer in charge of this column pulled up, blew a whistle, which caused the occupants of the jeeps to stop, dismount with browning machine guns on tripods and I was wondering what the hell was going on. Then some 12 machine guns opened up on the NFs on the hill. The NFs, thinking the Chinese had got behind them started down the hill. The Yanks, seeing the men coming down the hill, took them for Chinese and carried on firing. I smartly traversed my gun on the column of Yanks and shouted down to the Officer in charge. 'Get the hell out of here or I'll blast you out'. My gun was trained on the column. The Officer blew his whistle. The firing ceased, they remounted their jeeps swung round and left. The NFs had, by now, vacated the hill so I dismounted, contacted the Major and prepared to shoot him back on the hill, but the Chinese had taken advantage of this stupid error and attained the top of the hill in force, and laying on the blind side of the hill so I couldn't knock them off. We tried three times, I fired at the top of the hill keeping the Chinks down, but when the NFs got to the top, the Chinks came up and pushed them down. There was nothing I could do, so in conjunction with the Major in charge, the NF took up other defensive positions and I kept the Chink's heads down. The NFs never took that hill again … thanks to our friends the Yanks.

As darkness fell, the tanks were withdrawn into a leaguer, there to clean the guns, fill up with petrol, replenish the ammo, make a meal and try to get some sleep; but few of us got any sleep that night. The Infantry were getting attacked again, the shooting was getting closer and heavier, so I, like the rest of the tank crews, sat in my tank trying to nod off. Before dawn we were up, making tea and breakfast and at first light we set off again to the aid of our friends.

I was sent off to a different Company of NFs who had been attacked all night. When I got into position I weighed up the situation and I saw aircraft recognition panels on the top of a hill where the NF were entrenched. There was some fighting going on up there and the situation was somewhat confused. I got down from my tank and contacted an Officer of the NFs who explained the situation as he knew it and he pointed out that the aircraft panel was where the NF were holding, but to the East were Chinks; so I sent up a marker making sure I was on the right target, then I tried to dislodge the Chinese, but they were swarming up the far side of the hill and the NFs were gradually getting pushed off. The Company Commander came down and put me in the picture, so with his help I fired his men onto another feature, then when all his men were clear of the original hill, I called for an air strike, giving full instruction that the aircraft panel on the hill to be bombed should be ignored, as the Chinese were using it for their own protection.

The fighters flew in and dropped napalm bombs' all over the hill setting it on fire, I also shelled the approaches to the hill from the East. During these two days the Gloucesters were taking one hell of a hammering from all sides. A troop of tanks was dispatched to assist them but the terrain and a broken down Philippino tank thwarted any attempt to break through to help the Gloucesters. A main feature in this battle was the mountain called Kamak San. This feature overlooked the whole valley that we were trying to keep open for the Infantry. From it the Chinese were able to bring fire on the NF wherever they were, but after numerous air strikes they would not be dislodged so the situation became grim. Strenuous efforts were made to get the Gloucesters but to no avail.

In the late afternoon, a regiment of American Sherman tanks passed through us on their way to help the Belgians, then the Gloucesters. I felt relief at the sight of all this armour, so I cheered them on their way. One Tank Commander shouted at me 'We'll get it done for you, buddy.' In my ignorance I thought they just might. As dusk was falling the tanks once again began to pull out for their leaguer area. I was posted in a position where I could see down the valley and the position of the Royal Ulster Rifles. There I was to stay as a rearguard to the Squadron. As the last tank went out of sight, the Chinks started to throw mortars at me. At this moment, I felt very lonely. I could see the occasional flash but as the light was now fading, I couldn't see whether it was ours or theirs. I could just about make out the shape of Kamak San when I was ordered to withdraw. With great relief I told my driver to start up and we moved off in the direction of our leaguer area. The Chinks were still throwing mortars at us but as I went back they stopped.

Although I was relieved at getting out my thoughts were with the P.B.I. on those hills with Chinks all around them. I knew they were going to get hell when it got dark, in spite of the American tanks that had gone to their aid. We all knew that tomorrow would be a bad day because the Chinese had been infiltrating behind us and they were everywhere. They were getting slaughtered but it didn't seem to bother them, they just kept coming. Imagine, a line of ants crossing a garden path, you put your foot on that line and kill all under your foot. When you lift your foot the ones that didn't get trodden on just carry on in a straight line as though nothing had happened. That is just how the Chinks behaved. This was soul destroying to men like me who had fought the Italians and Germans and see them go to ground when you open up on them.

When I reached the leaguer area I was greeted by our CO and Squadron Leader, Major Huth, who had flown back from Japan. The usual routine of gun cleaning, filling up with petrol and ammo and any maintenance the driver may have to do was done then tea and food, then sleep. I hadn't had a wash or shave for three days, nor had I slept much. I didn't anticipate much sleep that night because I knew that the Chinese weren't far away. Four a.m. and we were up and making tea and eating biscuits. There was thick fog but by 5 a.m. we were off to another day of killing.

As on our usual route to the valley, we had to by-pass a small bridge, but this morning the detour was full of Chinese so the leading troop had to fight its way through the ambush; having cleared that obstacle, I knew my guess of the day before was going to prove correct, that the Chinks had infiltrated the whole of the valley, so our task to hold the road open for the Infantry to get out was going to be very problematical. We had to fight our way back to the positions of the day before. Two tanks went off the track, one of them threw a track, they were stuck there for a while being sniped at. I went on up to where the Ulsters and NFs were, only to find the place overrun with Chinks, having cleared the immediate area, I positioned myself where I could watch Kamak San and the approaches to the valley from that area. At about 7 a.m. I saw a Private of the NFs wandering about, lost, so knowing full well that this chap was dead beat having been fighting for three days and nights, I called him over. I told him to get up on my tank, which he did with pleasure.

Then I gave him my bren gun with several magazines and told him to stay put and watch my rear. If any Chinks showed themselves, shoot them. He appeared only too pleased to do this as he felt safe. So with my backside covered I was able to concentrate on my front. I saw hundreds of Chinamen crawling all over Kamak San, which was 1200 yards away, well within range on my gun and possibly in range on my Besa machine gun, so I was in for a good shoot. I saw a file of Chinese working their way down the mountainside so I directed my gunner on to this file. When he said that he was on target, I checked through his telescope, only to find he was on another file, slightly higher up, so I told him to fire at his target. I fired for what appeared to be hours. I stopped some of them, but after a while, they came again.

At about 9 a.m. I decided it was time we had a cup of tea, so my driver, who had been spotting for me from his position in front, got out the necessary, went round to the back of the tank where he was pretty well protected and brewed up. This brew up was much appreciated, especially by our infantryman friend on the back.

Then I spotted a group about platoon strength on the flat working their way round to the South West of our position. These were quickly disposed of with H.E. I didn't see any further movement in that area. After about three hours of continual firing, my machine gun barrels needed changing; my recoil system was so hot that it wouldn't run back and my loader-cum-operator Ken Hall, had fainted with the continual hard work and fumes. I got on the blower (radio) for a refill of ammo. Captain Murray obliged. I had revived my loader who took a short rest whilst I myself and the driver loaded the ammo and I changed the barrel of the Besa. My Fusilier friend had several bursts at three Chinks who popped up from a trench some 300 yards to the rear and he settled their hash. During this lull in firing the Chinks were still coming on and the range I gave my gunner was down to 800 yards, so off we went again. This time I could see more clearly the damage I was doing, especially with my machine gun. Where I could I gave my loader a break and so long as my gunner had targets to shoot at, I would do a bit of loading, whilst Ken Hall stuck his head out of the turret to get some fresh air. Of course we had noticed that the bushes were moving closer, ever closer, so the occasional burst sent them further away.

The order had been given for all of the Infantry units to get out of the valley, so it was our job to see them safely out. They started to come through our position. I could have cried at the state of some of those lads. Tired, dirty and no doubt hungry. If I live to be a hundred I shall never forget this pathetic sight of our poor lads plodding back. Their march back was by no means over once they passed us as the track to our South was cut off and crawling with Chinese. In order to by-pass this trap, many of the troops took to the hills East of us. I kept my guns firing and once again I got on the blower and asked for more ammo. Captain Murray brought me a limited amount and whilst my crew were loading up I gave him a sitrep (situation report) of what was going on in my immediate area. He agreed with me that the situation was gradually getting out of hand because no matter what was thrown at the Chinese they just kept coming, although I was keeping them at bay.

My Fusilier on the back had an occasion to use his bren gun. It appears that the Chinks were trying to get round the back of us and to encircle the tanks guarding the valley, but his watchful eye put paid to that move. At about midday things began to go wrong. Again my big gun refused to run back from the recoil, my Besa M/G was 'key-holing'* and I was running out of ammo again.

I got on the air to the Squadron Leader and put him in the picture regarding my situation. He told me to bring my Second Troop Sergeant into my position, see him on to my targets, then pull out and go back to where Brigade Headquarters was the night before. I carried out his orders. I saw Sergeant Holberton on to my targets, then pulled out onto the road. Now I knew that I was going to run into trouble on my way back, so I instructed my gunner and operator to make available my hand grenades and their side arms, because my tank was no longer a fighting vehicle. On the track were lots of the Infantrymen, all absolutely beat, so I picked up as many as I could possibly carry. Now, although I didn't give it much thought at the time, I have since and I still don't know if I did right picking up these men, knowing I was going to have to run the gauntlet through the Chinese who had infiltrated through to our rear. I suppose I thought that the passengers could fire at anyone who tried to interfere with our progress. Unfortunately, this was not the case. The Chinese were quite thick on either side of the track and they fired at close range at the Infantrymen on my tank, killing quite a few.

Then I had to negotiate the trap which we came through earlier in the morning. As I approached this trap I could see the Chinese swarming down in the detour I was due to take, so I ordered my driver to cross the bridge; this bridge was the cause of the detour, it wasn't thought strong enough to hold the weight of a tank. However, I told my driver to cross the bridge as fast as he could in order that the weight of the tank was not long enough on the bridge to cause it to collapse, nor to weaken it. As I crossed the bridge I lobbed four grenades into the trap which reduced the opposition. We did it O.K. and when I was clear of the trap I stopped. I asked the passengers to roll off the dead, and we then picked up some more weary stragglers. I got going again and again I saw Chinks coming down from he hills. A Captain of the NF who was sitting on my nearside front mudguard was firing rapid fire at targets in every direction. I tossed two grenades at a group by the track and my passengers were keeping up their spirits by having a go. In this way my tank became quite a formidable fighting vehicle, but this didn't stop some of them getting hit by concentrated enemy fire. The Captain of the NFs who was so bravely holding his own, caught a burst of machine gun fire across his midriff which made him sit down. It wasn't long before I came across a first aid post where I stopped and got the Captain and any other wounded off for treatment. There was still some firing coming from the hills, so I picked up some more passengers and drove on for another mile where I considered it was safe to drop them. I reported my position to my Squadron Leader who told me to stop there until I received further orders. Gradually, throughout the late afternoon other tanks from my Squadron joined me. One thing I couldn't understand was how my

Second Sergeant, Sergeant Holberton, was, within an hour of my departure, captured.

On my way back down the track I saw our M.O. who was captured, surrounded by Chinamen. I had no means of assisting him because the passengers on my tank at this time were being shot and if I had stopped, all of them would have been slaughtered; so I had run the gauntlet at, I'm afraid, great cost. I often wonder if I hadn't picked up some of those men, would those who were killed on my tank, have survived and got back under their own steam? These queries can never be answered. I did hear that the Captain who was shot whilst on my tank recovered and returned to England.

Gradually, the Squadron gathered and the Squadron Leader, who ended up holding open the valley with one other tank, met up with us in the evening and we moved back to a leaguer area where we replenished with petrol and ammo, whilst I waited earlier on my gunner doing some maintenance on the big gun and managed to get it right.

So ended the Battle of the Imjim. The Chinks seemed to give up after the hammering they had taken. In the leaguer area that night there were many stories to be told, how various chaps dealt with their different circumstances. All did their part in stemming the flow of Chinese which enabled the Infantrymen to get back safely out of that valley of death.

The next morning the Squadron moved back to the Seoul area but one of my troop tanks had mechanical trouble which was being attended to by the fitters. Being as we were not very far from the battle area, I stayed behind to assist should it become necessary. By the afternoon we had all rejoined the Squadron, there to relax for a few days.

CHAPTER 26

Civvy Street beckons

It became apparent to me that we had quite a number of men in the Squadron who could play a mouth organ, so I gathered them together and I formed a mouth organ band. On one particular night we had a get-together around a fire, nearly all of the Squadron turned up including Officers. There was plenty of beer and my band performed very well. We had a really good night which went on until the early hours; then some days later, I arranged a football match between a Company of NFs at which I officiated as Referee. The pitch wouldn't have passed inspection elsewhere, but ours was good enough to give the lads a good game, which we lost 3-2. Then some time later I was lucky enough to get to Japan on four days R. & R. (rest and recuperation). Now this was something else!

When I knew I was going to Tokyo, I got in touch with an American acquaintance who gave me an address of a good hotel in Tokyo where, as he said, everything was laid on. This R&R service was laid on by the Americans, so it was from an American Airbase that we flew to Japan. Once there I had to report to a British base, then off for four days. So I called up a taxi and went straight to the hotel given to me by my

American friend. Here I soon learnt about some of the Japanese customs. Once I got in I was given a room then I was ushered out by a beautiful girl who took me to a 'Bathroom', which bore no resemblance to a bathroom as I knew it. I disrobed – or I was disrobed – and given a bath, having been washed all over I was invited to get into what I can only describe as an old-fashioned copper, where I rinsed down in almost boiling water. I got out of that in something of a hurry and I was soon smothered in towels, dried off by the same beautiful girl, then offered a kimono; this I grabbed to cover my embarrassment. I was then taken to a room where I saw a spread which I had only seen in the pictures. My young lady was still with me. I tucked into a meal but I didn't know what I was eating. It was good whatever it was! Having eaten my fill, a glass of saki, which I didn't like, then I went back to my room where I dressed to go out for the night. I found I was only a short distance from the 'Ghinza' the Bond Street of Tokyo. I went to the American PX where I had some presents sent home to my wife – some beautiful Japanese silks and china, then I went to see a show which was presented for the Americans.

The four days went too quickly so it was a plane back to Kimpo Airfield and to the War, I was in a party which carried out a particularly nasty job, but a necessary one.

We went back to the battle area of a few weeks before to find the dead wherever they might be found. When a body was found it was identified if possible then the remains were put into a blanket for removal to a proper grave in an official cemetery. Whilst we carried out this task we were given a double rum ration.

The 28th Brigade joined us and so the First British Commonwealth Division was formed, so we were withdrawn from the 29th Brigade and became the Divisional Armoured Regiment and instead of one Squadron per Regiment, it was now one Squadron per Brigade. This, to a Tank Regiment, was more in keeping with the role they were used to. We were now in the rainy season so the building of 'Bashas' (structures of wood and straw in which we could shelter from the continuous rain) was the order of the day. We were not moving about much so we settled down in our Bashas. We were, at this time, going on recces and small actions, because Peace talks had started up. Hopes were high that some agreement may be reached. Major Huth, my Squadron Leader, remembering that I was once a trumpeter, asked me if I could blow the 'Cease Fire' should the order come through. If he could get me a trumpet I would be only too pleased to do so, was my reply. However, the order didn't come through and was not due to come through for some time yet.

Over these past few months my letters from my wife were getting fewer and fewer. I was beginning to have misgivings, then by October they stopped coming altogether, so I applied through SSAFFA (Soldiers Sailors and Air Force Families Association) for an explanation. Eventually, I had an answer back and a recommendation to return home. I made my application and on my birthday on 2nd November, I was granted a passage home. The day before some 90 men of the 5th Inniskillen Dragoon Guards arrived, the vanguard of our relieving Regiment. I flew home on a B.O.A.C. flight and once I arrived in England it didn't take me long to sort out my domestic troubles. Having been granted two weeks leave I got things all ship-shape and then reported to our advance party which had arrived and was settling in at Perham Downs. Whilst they went on leave, I started to organise the Regimental Orderly Room and I worked all hours getting the Regiments leave passes and train tickets ready for their arrival.

They arrived back home on 14th January and they got down to Tidworth by the evening. The next morning they were sent on six weeks' leave. I continued working in the Orderly Room until the Regiment came back from leave then I returned back to my Squadron. Then, for some unknown reason, I seemed to fall out with my Regiment. The Regiment was due to go to B.O.A.R. in March, but I wasn't going with them.

Bearing in mind that in the past I had been a radio operator, and a tank gunner, and a gunnery instructor, I was somewhat taken aback when my C.O. told me that I was going to Bovington R.A.C. Depot on a Driving and Maintenance Instructors Course; a subject I knew very little about. I knew that when one goes on an Instructors Course one had to have a good knowledge of the subject, sufficient to pass an entrance exam. This I knew was out of the question. I told this to my C.O. but he said that he would get me in, which in fact he did. As for the Course, whereas all the other students knew their subject very well, it was all above my head and I was way behind, but I tried and swotted. I didn't go out once during the Course, but at the final exam I just failed to get the pass marks.

The Regiment sent me up to York as an Instructor to the Yorkshire Hussars. In my own mind I knew I wasn't capable to instruct the maintenance of tanks. Now, if it had been gunnery or wireless, I could cope, but I was supposed to instruct on a subject I had scant knowledge of. I felt I had been done wrong and I had been on several other Courses and passed with flying colours, but to fail shook my confidence. I felt I had let both myself and my Regiment down. I was then posted to Warkop, a tank gunnery range, not as an instructor but as a permanent Sergeants' Mess Caterer. This was certainly a come down for me. I was losing my place in the Regiment which I had served for nearly 20 years. I could not understand why.

After a year at Warkop I applied to return to my Regiment at Luneburg. This was eventually granted, so my wife and son accompanied me to Luneberg, where I went back to 'C' Squadron and into a tank. This was more like it.

I did my month as Sergeant' Mess Caterer, then back into the tank troop. The Regiment were carrying out training and firing on Hohne ranges then from out of the blue I was sent for by the C.O. who told me I was being sent home on an E.R.E. (Extra Regimental Employed) posting to, of all places, the Army Apprentice School at Harrogate. This sickened me, as I was now settled down to the Regimental routine. I now knew that I was being ostracised, but why I did not know.

I was sent to Harrogate as a general dogsbody, to complete the permanent staff establishment. I was soon put on a cadre and obtained top marks on small arms and drill and although I was out of place here with Guards CSMs and Infantry WOs and Sergeants, I was determined not to let the Cavalry down. The Army Apprentice School is a Military School for boys between the ages of 15 and 18, learning military trades, such as engineering trades for the Royal Engineers, gunnery for the Royal Artillery and signals for the Royal Corps of Signals. These subjects were taught by instructors from the various units and my job was to instruct the military side, such as the use of small arms and drill and the normal military admin. duties.

My past record of sport and of officiating at sports came in very handy as sport was very much on the school curriculum and they had all the necessary sports fields and equipment. There was much rivalry between the Companies on the sports field and also between the other Apprentice School at Chepstow and Arborfield and the RAF boys' school; so I soon settled down to the ways of a boys' school. The Commandant was Colonel Carne, V.C. of the Gloucesters, with whom we had fought in Korea. I was posted to 'D' Company and I soon got to know the boys and they soon got to know me. My boots were a talking point among them because I kept them like a glass and soon they were all trying to match them, so I passed on a few tips, which helped to get them the Best Turned-Out Company Award.

The CSM from the Scots Guards went sick and I took his place, competing as it were with other Guards CSMs. I retained this job for four weeks so I got paid for it. Whilst I was carrying out the duties of CSM, I got to know the Company Commander very well. He was an infantry officer and when he learnt that I was well up on army accountancy he enlisted my aid to help him complete his accounts for the Audit Board and we got on very well.

I knew my hopes of promotion within my Regiment were now non-existent and I also knew that so long as I was on the

ERE list I couldn't get promoted, otherwise I would be taking on promotion from the establishment of the Regiment and that could never be done, so I had to be contented with my lot as a member of the permanent staff of the Army Apprentice School. I had a good married quarter right on the edge of the sports field. I was soon elected to the School's Sports Committee and as I was the senior army referee in the Harrogate district I was elected to the Harrogate and District Referees' Committee; so I was kept busy on the sports fields.

The CQMS of our Company suffered from ulcers so when he went into hospital for an operation I was instructed to take over his job. This sort of work suited me very well as quite a lot of it was bookwork. I carried out this job for about six weeks when Jock the CQMS returned. Then a new establishment was formed at the School. This entailed the formation of a Permanent Staff Company. Whereas in the past all permanent staff were attached to the various Companies with whom they worked, now they had a Company of their own. I was given the duties of SQMS with the temporary rank. I carried out this job to the satisfaction of all and at the end of three months I was entitled to a substantive rank of SQMS but because I was still on the ERE list of the 8th Hussars, this did not appear possible. However, Colonel Carne, V.C. called me into his office and put it to me that if I was struck off the 8th Hussars strength I could become substantive on the RAC list. He said that in his opinion I merited the promotion and he was only too pleased to grant me it. So I became a substantive SQMS. How strange, I thought, that the 8th Hussars wouldn't recognise my abilities when someone else would!

I was nominated to referee the Army Cup Final at Catterick between the Royal Corps of Signals and the RTR. The Signals at this time was full of professionals doing their national Service. It was an easy match to referee as both sides showed standards of sportsmanship, which one always got in service matches. The result was a win for the Signals 2-1. Then the next big sporting event was the introduction of the Youth Club Series and the Army Apprentice School Harrogate was chosen as the venue for the first match. They played a representative team from Yorkshire at which Sir Stanley Rouse attended. I was the referee and another good game was played. The School won by the only goal and Sir Stanley issued commemorative medals to both teams and the officials. I took over the running of the P.S. team and we were entered for two cups and the Harrogate & District Senior League.

The year of 1956 was a very successful season for both the boys and the P.S. The School won three cups and the P.S. won the League.

Then I nearly died. I was feeling pain in my stomach and not being one for reporting sick unless it was absolutely necessary, the pain persisted for some days and eventually I did report sick and after an examination the MO pronounced a grumbling appendix – so back to duty. The pain was so bad that I took myself off to bed. Then, later on in the late afternoon, the pain was so bad that I could not even lie down in comfort, so I asked my wife to call in the M.O. who came and gave me another examination and said 'I must get you into Catterick Military Hospital', which was some sixty miles away. I told him that I wouldn't make it there so he then tried to get me into the Harrogate Infirmary. By about six o'clock in the evening I was taken by ambulance to the Harrogate Infirmary and when I got there I walked into the ward and when the doctor saw me walking he threw a fit and immediately called for a stretcher. I was operated on for appendicitis within the hour, but when the doctors got inside me they told me that the appendix had burst causing peritonitis and I was put on the D.I. (dangerously ill) List. The Commandant (Colonel Carne, V.C.) came to visit me as did lots of other Officers and men and boys. Thanks to good nursing I recovered completely.

Of course, all this happened whilst I was under a threat of a serious charge. I had knocked down two drunks who had walked straight at my car from the sidewalk and as it was after closing time at night there were no witnesses, until at the inquest a couple came forward to say that they were driving a car on that same stretch of road at about the same time and they had narrowly missed the two pedestrians who were wandering drunkenly in the middle of the road. I was cleared of any negligence or dangerous driving, although the man involved died of his injuries.

About this time there was talk in the air of amalgamation of the 8th Hussars with the 4th Hussars. This was the death knell of two famous Cavalry Regiments. Both were to loose their individual titles and their own traditions, cherished over the centuries. To an 8th Hussar, such as I, it didn't seem justified. The Colonel-in-Chief, the Colonel of the Regiment and the Commanding Officer all fought against this decision. All three had fought some terrific battles in their time, on battlefields throughout the world and sometimes against great odds, but together they couldn't win this one.

So it was that in October 1958 the 4th and 8th Hussars went into oblivion and the Queen's Royal Irish Hussars were born.

Although I was not immediately affected, as I was on the staff of the A.A.S. Harrogate, I kept in close touch with my Regiment as I had many friends who wrote to me. At the time of the amalgamation I felt a pang of sadness as I had been an 8th Hussar for nearly 25 years. As always, two good Cavalry Regiments, both very adaptable, soon learned to live with the decision and very soon the Queen's Royal Irish Hussars was an efficient unit, second to none.

At the end of 1959 I decided to retire from the Army, having completed 28 years, man and boy. Finally, it was my turn to say "Civvy Street, here I come!"

The Author, 1992.